LIFE IS A CIRCUS RUN BY A PLATYPUS

Surviving a Normally Surreal Life

by Allison Hawn

13 digit ISBN: 978-1512025491
10 digit ISBN: 1512025496

Published in the United States of America

Interior Design by Craig A. Hart
Cover Design by Paul Brand
Front Cover Art by Anthony Carpenter

To Annie Larlee who kept me alive,
Mom, Dr. Glena Andrews and Dr. Donna Allen for telling me
what to do with my life,
And to Anne Seil, Mollie Hunt, Amanda Konzal and Kari
Chapman for balancing the rest.

Chapters

1. AN INTRODUCTION TO INSANITY

A belly-dancing Wiccan recently informed me that my life is bizarre. Granted, family and friends have been telling me this for years, but I think it really hit me in the face, like a confused and directionally challenged eagle, when that same sentiment was expressed by someone who semi-frequently dresses as a woodland nymph and dances around fires. As another friend described it, "You are like a magnet for weird."

Not only is my life bizarre, it's downright mad. Now that I finally believe what others have been telling me for years, I will admit defeat and I will do what several of them have requested of me: That I write about it.

There are several realizations I have come to of late. First, I will never be an Olympic figure skater. Second, I will probably never understand exactly how Jell-O works. Finally, even the weirdest situations can yield some important lessons.

For instance, I once lived in what used to be a classy Idaho neighborhood. Ok, I realize that putting "Idaho" and "classy" in the same statement means I might as well have said, "I used to do a 'classy' show in the basement of a bar named Bud's Eats." But work with me here, rich, or at least richer, people used to live there 40 years ago.

Today, the neighborhood is a conglomeration of rentals, private nursing home type situations and a few tough nosed neighbors who like the placement of their plastic flamingo collections too much to move. My old neighborhood was dangerous in the, "If aliens were to abduct someone, it would most likely happen here," kind of way.

Let me give you an example. One evening I was walking my family's two-pound sort-of dog around what still appeared to be the nice suburban neighborhood. As I wandered I was caught in a tunnel vision of identical houses, a visual monotony only broken by the occasional garden gnome and my dog straining with all his tiny might to go where he pleased. It was hypnotizing, like watching an infomercial at three in the morning for one of those ladders that can bend into ninety-five different shapes.

As I strolled by a nice little grey house, tacky front lawn ornaments included, I happened to look inside the open garage. The cement-lined space was virtually empty except for a few boxes and a woman dressed in a green Christmas sweater and unlaced hiking boots who also was carrying a rifle, scope attached. Wandering around her garage, looking down the barrel of her weapon and muttering something that sounded incredibly like, "I'm gonna get ya."

I wasn't entirely sure whether she had forgotten to take her medication, or had taken far too much of it.

There was a brief moment when I wondered if I had managed to get a dose of acid without my knowledge while I was walking, but then I realized this was too bizarre for drugs. I'm not exactly sure what the lady was hunting in her garage, but far be it from me to question her methods.

As I briefly paused, staring like a cow looks at an oncoming semi, the woman spun towards me and my dog, gun still pointed at the ground in front of her. "Did you see it!?"

I had no more clue of what "it" was than a baby has any idea what it would do with a tangoing weasel. In fear for my life, I simply smiled, shook my head and tried to look more apologetic than Bill Clinton. The woman snapped back towards her garage and continued her hunt, her interest in me completely gone.

I must say, I may not have stuck around to tell her this as I jackrabbit ran to put distance between myself and her home, but I did admire her initiative. Whatever was in her garage had definitely foiled her for the last time and she was determined to get the job done, or accidentally redecorate the interior of her home trying.

Either way, this was a take-charge, getting her way, probably started drinking at noon kind of woman. There are some lessons to be learned from this paragon of efficiency.

1. We should never forget that if we try hard enough and carry the right equipment we can solve any problem.

2. We should also never forget that it is probably not a good idea to cut our morning orange juice with Liquid Drano too.

2. PETS AND OTHER PERILS

Occasionally I have had friends ask me to watch their pets while they are out of town, in the hospital or taking clogging lessons in Norway. Often, the conversation goes something like this:

Other person: "Can you watch Mr. Scruffles for a couple days? He's super easy to handle and is the nicest, sweetest, most George Clooney-like cat/dog/field mouse/chinchilla/lizard bigger than your toddler cousin ever!"

Me: "What does that entail?"

Other person: "Oh, nothing. Just pour his food in his bowl and let him out to pee/clean his cage and he will be a perfect little angel."

How they describe the favor makes it sound like I will spend happy hours cuddling with a magical creature who has the disposition of Mother Teresa. Of course I agree to watch Mr. Scruffles.

Now, there are some animals I have watched who have been little bundles of fur and joy wrapped up in rainbows. The wide majority of those I have pet-sat, however, appear to have come straight from the bowels of elevator music hell.

The first red flag is when you show up so that the owner can show you what your responsibilities concerning the critter will be, and they begin saying, "Oh! I forgot to mention..."

Sometimes this is something easy and silly like, "I forgot to mention that Mr. Scruffles snores."

What it usually ends up being is something like, "I forgot to mention that Mr. Scruffles can only eat food that's been cooked in a ceramic bowl made by Romanian Monks and warmed to exactly 94 degrees (and no, they won't say whether they mean Fahrenheit or Celsius) and prayed over by a Voodoo priest or he'll throw up on your pillow at four in the morning."

Let me give you an example: I once pet-sat for some people who had a golden retriever, two chinchillas and an iguana which was easily the size of one of my arms. The walk-through, which was supposed to take, "Five minutes tops, I promise," took nearly

3

an hour as the phrase, "Oops, I don't think I mentioned..." began to threaten my grip on reality.

I was informed that the iguana's tank temperature had to be measured bi-hourly at night, the chinchillas habitually dismantled their cage so I needed to make sure they stayed in their habitat and the dog would get nervous if left alone too long and thus either eat the sofa or do something indescribable on the carpet (and I wasn't allowed to scold the dog because, "He doesn't know what he's doing is wrong").

To my chagrin, I couldn't back out at this point because the owners were to leave the next day for some adventure in the Sahara Desert, or to some other such place where the only way to contact them would be via camel mail. So I set out to tame the jungle armed with carpet cleaner and enough chinchilla food to last a lifetime.

The first couple of days went well enough until the day I had to go to work. Five hours later I came back to find... well... imagine that instead of using bullets, the soldiers in the Civil War had fought with feces. The term "holy shitstorm" did not even begin to describe the mess as all the walls were bespeckled with tiny turds.

What the owners forgot to bring up was that the chinchillas not only figured out how to occasionally dismantle their cage, but if they failed to do that, they then resorted to throwing poop from in between their bars in protest of their captivity.

I think these chinchillas needed to be drafted in the NFL, they were able to pitch poop and hit the wall across the room with enough force that it stuck there.

How do I know it was the chinchillas doing this? Because right when I walked in they propelled a volley at the golden retriever, startling it so much that he ran around yipping and trampling anything in its path, including the volcano sized land mines of poop that he had strategically laid out that day.

I eventually got the dog outside (where he pretty much lived until the owners got home), and then I leaned a piece of wood against the chinchillas' cage bars limiting their poop-flinging fun.

It wasn't until I was nearly done cleaning I realized that I still had yet to feed the gigantic lizard. The entire time I had been Keeper of the Zoo, I had yet to see the iguana move. It sat in the same position it had when I first saw it a week ago. Already tired, I got his pellets and lifted the lid to dump some in for the rock with eyes.

I peered down at the tank in just enough time to see the iguana blink and then, like a cold-blooded, land crawling, version of Moby Dick, he leaped towards the top of his aquarium home.

He got half of his body out of the tank before I smacked the lid down on top of him, which I think stunned him enough to give me time to do something useful; namely toss the food up in the air while yelling something along the lines of, "Holy tap-dancing Marlon Brando!"

The way I'd like to portray what happened next would be the heroic battle between Allison and the Giant Iguana, much like that of Saint George and the Dragon (armor and spear included). What actually happened is that I got a really big book of fairy tales lifted the lid of the tank and proceeded to swat the iguana on the nose hard enough to get the mighty beast to thud heavily back in its cage like an off-balance sumo wrestler hitting the mat.

This is a cautionary tale and there are some valuable lessons to be learned:

1. When it comes to pets, know what you are getting yourself into. Sure, you could end up with an adorable puppy that cuddles and practically farts smiles, but then again you could end up with poop-armed chinchillas with excellent aim and the surprise pouncing iguana.

2. Make sure that the owners of the pet you are watching buy extra carpet cleaner and, depending on the pet, possibly a battle-axe before they leave town.

3. IDIOTS AND THEIR USES

Oh the ways that we pay for education. I'm positive that most of the people we think of as geniuses and paragons of society had to have some crappy little side job until they could get their credentials.

I can see a young Joan of Arc advertising the wares of a local jam seller by dressing up in a festive outfit, a teenage Winston Churchill cleaning Parliament's bathrooms or a juvenile Aristotle shoveling out Pegasus' stable. And I will bet every single one of them had a coworker who made them lose just a tad bit of faith in the whole of the human race.

I have had a plethora of summer jobs in the futile endeavor of trying to keep myself from drowning in debt. Of course the economy, in some form of sadism matched only by someone forcing small children to watch a *Knight Rider* marathon, tanked just in time for me to get a summer job before my sophomore year of college. This is how I found myself one summer working at a Subway located in the middle of a trucker stop.

Yes, this means that I spent my days wearing a shirt advertising, "Five dollar foot-longs," as my blonde ponytail stuck out behind a visor, while selling sandwiches mostly to a group of people whose teeth to tattoo ratio was not in their favor.

I'm not exactly sure what the most ridiculous part of this job was: Getting hit on by people easily old enough to remember when the Titanic sank, wearing a tennis visor, which is intended to block out the sun, indoors, or the fact that several customers had most likely never seen the inside of a shower. I can say, however, that the most annoying part of that particular job was not so much of a what, but a who.

I had a coworker who, to put it accurately, had about as many working brain cells as a flaming owl pellet. For purposes of confidentiality we will call this person Dimwit, or D.W. for short. D.W. was introduced to me by the well-intentioned manager just before she realized that one of the machines in the back was making a funny noise and needed to be hit with a wrench again.

She had been gone no more than three seconds when D.W. turned his beady eyes on me and asked, "You got any extra dough on ya?"

With my negative answer D.W. threw his skinny arms in the air "Damn it all, how am I supposed to go to a strip club if I don't got any dollar bills!?"

This spun me for a loop, much like the ones on a three hundred foot roller coaster that is being operated by a group of oversized belligerent termites. This guy, who I had just met no longer ago than it takes for person to make a turkey and jalapeño sandwich, was asking me for stripper money.

I was also caught for a second by a couple of other rather important factors. Namely, D.W. was 16 or 17, and therefore not actually old enough to get into a strip club. Furthermore, he asked me, a *female*. Granted those uniforms are unisex, but I have long blonde hair, I wear make-up and probably most noticeably, I have *boobs*.

I have been exposed to idiots throughout my lifetime, from the person in their 20's who asked me who George Washington was, to the guy in my high school senior class who could not consistently spell his name correctly, but D.W. was a completely different class of idiot.

The entire first day I worked with D.W., he kept bragging about how he had spent some hard time in prison. Finally, annoyed into showing interest in this banal fact, I asked him how long he was in prison. This is when I found out that by "prison" he actually meant "jail," and by "hard time" he meant "two days."

It turns out that D.W. had some pot, which a friend stole. D.W., somehow briefly grasping the concept of personal ownership, had called the police to report his fair-weathered friend's horrible crime. D.W. was baffled as to how the cops got him on that possession charge, "They must have a psychic or something."

Now, for those of you who do not know the inner workings of a Subway, there are slow cooking bread ovens. Let me emphasize SLOW cooking. This oven, if pressed, could bake a mini-muffin in 30 minutes. It took the bread for sandwiches approximately the same amount of time it would take for an army of one legged turtles soaked in superglue to cross the Sahara desert to actually rise and bake.

The entire oven was operated by one switch, which offered the two often-confusing settings of "off" and "on." There was even a handy dandy self-setting timer that would let out a shrill sound, tantamount in its annoying qualities to the sound of a *Kidz Bop* album.

7

Readers at home may be thinking, "This sounds ridiculously easy to operate. I could have a toddler on children's cough syrup operate this oven."

I would first have to say to you, "No!" If you read the cough syrup label it clearly states that those under the influence of that particular drug should not operate heavy machinery. Having had to lift that oven at one point I can definitely attest to the fact that it is one heavy carbonized steel box.

Second, while one would think that there is no way in heaven or hell that someone could somehow manage to fail at operating this machine, it is clear that idiocy will find a way.

On one hot sticky afternoon while I was working with D.W., the food stock delivery came. Normally, when the stock arrives, we had at least three people in the store so that two people could attend the front while one unlucky bugger got to go spend countless hefting hours in a walk-in freezer trying to figure out where the hell to put another 35 pound box of unbaked cookie dough.

Unfortunately, the delivery was a day early, leaving it up to me and Captain Neanderthal to take care of the inventory. D.W. had all the capable lifting strength of a sleeping infant wombat, so I begrudgingly left him to manage the front counter and watch the baking bread while I hefted foodstuffs. It took me around an hour in the walk-in to get everything sorted and then delicately crammed into place.

When I emerged from my frozen cave, I was met by the familiar screeching cries of the 400-pound equivalent of an Easy-Bake Oven and the not as common smell of smoke. I rushed to the front of the store to find D.W. staring blankly at a smoking oven. D.W. had his head cocked slightly to the side, like a puppy that has just eaten the entire works of Sir Arthur Conan Doyle and is now confused as to why he's in trouble.

As he gazed into an abyss that refused to gaze back at him, I sprung into action. I quickly grabbed the oven mitts and fixed the problem, namely by throwing six trays of burnt bread outside, still smoldering like Freud's cigars.

In complete exasperation I asked, "How long was the timer going off for!?"

"Umm... well it started going off like 5 minutes after you went back..."

"Why didn't you take the bread out?"

D.W.'s face contorted into a "well duh" expression as he grunted, "Because that crap is hot!"

I held up the oven mitts, which had been resting on the counter no more than two inches from his left hand.

"Oh, yeah... I forgot about those."

I'm relatively sure I can trace the origins of my stress eye twitch to this moment.

Now, before my readers start thinking that I am a completely negative or pessimistic person, I must say there were some positives of working with a person who finds putting his shoes on the correct feet challenging.

Namely, D.W. was exceedingly easy to dupe into doing just about anything. Now, not only was this great for practical jokes involving doorways and saran wrap, but it served a practical purpose.

The summer I worked in this particular location boasted one of the hottest days on record. It also possessed the most road construction that area had seen in ten years. With temperatures outside well over a hundred, it was no surprise that several of the construction workers came in to enjoy the only air conditioning available to them as they grabbed a sandwich. This was mostly fine with me, particularly since some of those construction workers were mighty fine.

Before anyone curses me for ogling, let me say that all the good-looking, relief-seeking construction workers were balanced out by just *one* of their coworkers.

Possibly weighing in at just above The Incredible Hulk, but with none of the muscle, this wooly mammoth lumbered in.

His first action after stepping into the cool air of the trucker stop was to remove a shirt that already was failing at holding in a massive beer gut. The beer gut, though, was the least of my worries. The shirt removal revealed that this man was indeed related to King Kong, there was enough body hair to thatch the roofs of several African huts.

Now, for those who have lived in Amish country or under a pile of toenail clippings all their life, and therefore have never been to a Subway, there is this lovely glass shell covering the front part of the counter and curving above the food like some sort of sandwich topping shield. After I had just cleaned this window-like contraption, the customer jiggled over to me and then proceeded to lean against the glass as he ordered.

Have you ever seen when people, in attempt to be funny, or because they are being mugged, smash their faces up against windows? Now just imagine that with a beer gut and hairy man boobs. I'm sure the only thing that kept me from retching as I made his sandwich was the fact that I was in a state of shock.

As we moved down the sandwich-making line the man did not back away from the glass, instead he continued to lean and drag himself across the glass, leaving a slug-like slime trail behind him.

It was all I could do to not gouge my eyes out with the dull bread knife I was holding as I was slowly instructed to put nearly every topping we had on the sandwich.

He did not stand up until we reached the register at which point he had to leave his glass leaning post, which was accompanied by a loud sucking "SLURP!"

I made change faster than The Flash could run around a disabled Chevy Nova, and the missing link in the evolutionary chain left.

I stood, staring, bottom lip trembling, as the sweaty trail the man had left behind dripped down the glass towards the floor. My mind whirled, trying to find anything, any way that I wouldn't have to touch the sweat-trail that now glistened under fluorescent lights. Then, the idea hit me.

D.W. had been in the back attempting to cut vegetables, a task made complicated because the veggies he was supposed to be cutting kept getting away from him.

Calm and collected I went into the back of the shop and casually said, "D.W., I will cut every vegetable for prep if you will go out and clean the glass over the front counter."

A piece of tomato hopped off the chopping block and landed on the floor as D.W. gave one last hack to his vegetable victim. D.W. without questioning why I was willing to trade an hour of cutting onions, peppers and tomatoes for what is usually a ten-minute task happily agreed.

I quickly took over the knife, an implement I did not trust in D.W.'s hands anyways, and started in on the vegetables as D.W. grabbed the glass cleaner and headed for the front of the store. I had nearly chopped an entire pepper before he returned.

"Umm... what's all over the glass, and why does it smell like bacon?"

What morals can be learned from my experiences here?

1. Never clean any lean-able surface on the hottest day of summer.

2. Beware of idiots. There is a good chance that no matter how common sense-easy you believe a task to be, they will find a way to nearly burn you to death doing it.

3. If you are forced into confined quarters with an idiot for long amounts of time, use them as a helpful barrier against having to clean up others' bodily fluids.

4. REASON #435 I WILL NEVER HAVE KIDS

I am not really a kid person. I'm more of an "Awww that baby is adorable. Ok, what is that coming out of its nose? Ick, take it back, take it back," kind of person. I'm pretty sure all of my maternal genes were left under a bus seat when I lived in Georgia. However, as a teenager I had limited methods for making money, so I often acquiesced to babysitting.

I'm not sure what it is about me; maybe it was the amount of muscle I had, maybe it was my "take no crap" attitude, or maybe I was the only person available, but I attracted the most bizarre/dangerous/psychotic families to babysit for.

One such family called me up to babysit their three year and seven month old daughters. They told me that they had gotten my name from one of my friends.

I'm not sure when I made friends with the devil, but apparently I did, because that is the only entity I can think of who would be cruel enough to pass my name to these people.

My mom dropped me off at their cookie cutter two story house as the parents were walking out the front door. I could have been a burglar, random psychopath or the last living Candygram delivery girl, but this couple didn't seem to care. They booked it towards their car like they were being chased by a pack of wild rabid kangaroos as the mother yelled over her shoulder, "The kids are eating, they go to bed around 8, and the baby is sick!"

Then without so much as a, "Here's where you can reach us if the Apocalypse starts in our kitchen," they left in a flash of silver SUV and buzz of little kids sing-along tapes played at a decibel that rattled the windows.

With some trepidation, I entered the house, looking for the kitchen where the kids were supposedly eating. I wandered, calling out so that I would not scare the poop out of the children as I went, and eventually found the kitchen where the three year old was happily smearing chicken nuggets and ketchup in a rainbow pattern on the wall.

I introduced myself as best I could to the three year old, who regarded me with an expression denoting mommy and daddy had just brought home a new pet lizard. Obviously done eating, she decided to go to another room and play with her toys. The seven month old was strapped into a high chair, wearing only a diaper and contentedly beating her bottle against her trappings.

The baby didn't seem sick, but I still figured I'd stay on the safe side of things and take her to lie down. I went to pick her up, noting that she was a little warm and she began to cry. In an effort to calm her down I lifted her out of the high chair.

Big mistake. The baby was pressure-triggered. The second I lifted her out of the high chair, she exploded. At arm's length I watched in horror as the diaper struggled to contain the incoming tidal wave, like a tsunami bearing down on a pile of twigs, before giving up and unleashing the worst diarrhea I have ever seen.

I have no idea what the parents were feeding this kid, but if I had to hazard a guess, it would be enough refried beans, pureed sardines and demon spit to feed the entire cast and crew of the movie *300*.

There was baby poop everywhere, on the counter, the walls, the ceiling and, of course, me. The baby, relieved of approximately three tons of crap, stopped crying, giggled, and then threw up. It was at this point that, at 13 years old, I contemplated joining a nunnery so I could have religious reasons for never having children.

I was at a total loss as to what I should do. Thanks to the parents' hasty departure I didn't have the faintest hope of a clue as to where the nearest diaper, wet wipe or biohazard suit was. I looked at the clock, I had been there for about ten minutes.

It was at this point that my savior, standing at less three feet tall sauntered in and said, "Eeew, baby make mess."

Through a complicated simplification of my speech, with some elbow motions and interpretive dancing, I finally learned that the diapers were upstairs. I looked at the baby, who had been amusing herself by beating her bottle on my outstretched and tired arms. Waste was dripping off of the infant, and I had about 20 carpeted stairs and five yards of carpeted hall between me and the nearest diaper.

My solution? I carried the baby half encased in a garbage bag upstairs to take care of the situation.

The kids went to bed early that night, namely so I could start cleaning. If you have never gotten the chance to clean baby poop off of the ceiling let me give you a tip: Long handled paint rollers with a rag tied to the end is just about the only way to go.

Around midnight, after I had been in poop and vomit covered clothes for approximately a year and a half (or five hours if you want to split hairs), the parents staggered in. They took one look at me in my now vastly differently colored clothes, and then up at the remaining bits of baby droppings that I hadn't managed to get off the low ceiling, and then confusedly back to me. Obviously not putting two and two together in a way that did not come out to four-thousand, the mother asked, "Wha...?"

I raised my arms and gestured towards the baby created abstract art and said, "Oh, by the way, the baby is sick."

What tidbits can we take away from this?

1. Children excrete scary and dangerous substances, much like a leaking nuclear reactor. Wear appropriate protection. My vote: A biohazard suit with a raincoat over it.

2. If your kid is sick, don't pawn off the sickly one to a babysitter or you will officially qualify for the worst parent of the year award.

3. Wear clothes to babysitting jobs that you don't care if they are absolutely destroyed, because you will end up burning them later.

5. WATERLOGGED

Thud! Thud! Thud! "Charissa, I swear, if you don't get out of the bathroom there *will* be a puddle on your carpet!"

"Two puddles! Seriously, how long does it take to pee!?"

"That's it, I'm using the damn lawn!"

"We are no longer friends!"

That conversation not only happened, but nearly caused the downfall of several friendships in one swift motion, much like a panther pouncing on a startled dance production of *Stomp*.

Have you ever had a situation that you look back on and wonder, "Were we assaulted by mind deforming pixies when we decided to do that?"

That is the only reason I can think of why Charissa, Rachel and I would ever have thought of doing what we did on that fateful Saturday afternoon.

We were all more bored than a group of small children asked to watch a school PBS special. After all, we were attending college in Nampa, Idaho, which meant that there was about as much to do on a Saturday afternoon as there are intelligible words in any of Ozzy Osbourne's modern music.

All three of us scraped the innards of our very mental fortitude and imagination to find anything that might entertain us. As we sat there Rachel piped up, half jokingly, "Well, we could watch *Titanic*."

Since our alternatives at that point were to start a knitting circle or try to learn how to play the accordion in a group, we went for *Titanic*. I had not seen this movie since I was in about fourth grade when absolutely everyone in the world was so obsessed with it that I thought it might spawn its own religion.

Mostly remembering the hype and not the movie itself, I forgot several things about it. First, it is possibly one of the cheesiest films known to mankind. Second, the movie is really long.

After about fifteen minutes of watching my friends and I realized that this was boring us more than we had previously been. We looked for anything which could help us be entertained by the breathless Leonardo DiCaprio as he attempted to find passage on the ship.

I'm not sure who came up with the plan, maybe it was Satan whispering in our ears, but someone said, "Hey, why don't we turn this into a drinking game?"

Alcohol was out of the question, namely because we were all super poor and lived on a campus where there was a strict no booze policy. So we settled on taking a drink of water every time Rose's fiancé was a bastard, each instance where Jack said, "Rose," or Rose said, "Jack," and anytime someone needlessly jumped off of the sinking ship into the icy ocean water.

Armed with several gallons of water, we settled in to see who could earn the title of "iron bladder" since we all were determined to not use the restroom before the movie ended. That's right, this was a classy, classy ladies' afternoon.

The first hour went well enough. We diligently took gulps of water as Rose's fiancé would say things that made 1950's white men look positively progressive, and as the dialogue between Rose and Jack began to heat up towards relationship status.

If you have never seen *Titanic,* or it's been forever and a day, there is something I would like to point out: The directors and writers of this film were exceedingly worried about the audience forgetting the two main characters' names. As the film wore on, we discovered, in scenes between Rose and Jack, they used each other's names more often than one can find some form of fish that would gladly, given the chance, eat you in the ocean.

We all began to feel our bladders constrict as lines like, "Jack, I need you, Jack, to know, Jack, that I have to go, Jack, to the other end of the ship, Jack," popped up like evil gerbils on mini-trampolines throughout the film.

By the middle of the movie we were all sitting with our legs crossed so tight that I'm shocked our limbs didn't fuse together. Each of us was determined not to be the first one to give up and admit defeat in the face of bad acting and enough water to effectively drown ourselves.

Then, the ship sank. Not only did we count over 40 people who randomly were shown jumping into the water for no other reason than the director wanted it to seem more dramatic, but the dialogue between Jack and Rose became less and less of a conversation. Instead of meaningful sentences, the two main characters were reduced to shouting each other's names over and over and over.

"Jack!"

"Rose!"

"Jack!"

"Rose!"

"Jack!"

"Rose!"

Eventually we just gave up trying to count the names and started chugging water.

At this point we were watching the movie in "bouncy vision" as each one of us was hopping in our seat with more gusto than a nuclear powered Mexican jumping bean.

By the time Rose threw the Heart of the Ocean back into the depths of the sea we were crying, not because it was sad, but because each one of us felt like were about to explode in a manner worthy of a James Bond closing scene.

The credits rolled, and then there were two sudden realizations. The first one hitting us, like a yacht driven by yodeling yaks, was that we were now free to pee. The second... there was only one bathroom in the house.

We all made eye-contact and each one knew what the other was thinking, "Can I get up and run to the bathroom without wetting myself?"

The silence was absolute. One could've heard a piece of lint drop in the next-door neighbor's kitchen.

Suddenly, Charissa, the smallest of us all, leapt forth like a frog shot from a slingshot, "My house, my bathroom!" The bathroom door slammed shut while Rachel and I were left to resist using the kitchen sink to relieve our pain.

What can the waters of knowledge bring us?

1. Never, ever play any form of drinking game with a movie that takes longer to watch than it does to make a scarf out of string cheese.

2. If you do think about playing some form of drinking game (alcoholic or not), don't do it in a house with only one bathroom. Unless, of course, you really want to find out who your true friends are.

3. Drinking nearly a gallon of water in under three hours is a worse idea than trying to feed a tiger an apple while wearing a dress made out of lamb meat. It will hurt, a lot.

6. I HAVE TO FLOSS MY CAT
THAT NIGHT

I have held some pretty awesome jobs in my life thus far. I've helped train horses, worked at a small time newspaper and was a lighting technician for professional concerts. On the other end of that spectrum, I have also held jobs that smelled of burning dough, grease and shame.

I believe there is a special level of hell normally reserved for people who kick puppies or consistently say "lol" out loud instead of just laughing, requiring those who are ensnared to work at Little Caesar's Pizza for all eternity.

My first job out of high school and before college had me donning a dorky looking visor and a t-shirt that screamed, "Hot and Ready," across my chest in neon orange letters in a font that could easily be seen from Bavaria.

For an entire summer I showed up to stand under a lighted list providing customers with a cornucopia of food-like choices while kindly reminding them that, "Big or small, we service all!"

To say that I got hit on a few times is kind of like saying that juggling sticks of dynamite through a ring of fire while standing on top of a moving, pregnant alligator is only slightly dangerous. While the lame pick-up lines one would get from customers, like truckers, frat boys, one lady who was too high to remember that she was a straight, married female, were annoying as all get out, nothing could equal the advances made by my coworker, T(vowel)M.

I call him T(vowel)M because his name was either Tim or Tom, but despite my best efforts, I could never remember what his name actually was. If I actually had to refer to him, I usually said something like, "You in the visor who isn't Kirsten shaped..."

T(vowel)M was a 5'4" guy built of solid Cheetos and whipped cream eaten straight from the can. I'm relatively sure the only exercise he ever got was moving his fingers across his keyboard to look up the newest video game trailers. One could almost hear the acne in his voice.

The first time I met T(vowel)M, I had to work a six hour shift with him. During this shift, I made the mistake of mentioning that I had been involved with martial arts. This was the kind of mistake that could only be rivaled by the choice to let Pierce Brosnan sing in *Mamma Mia*.

T(vowel)M was a World of Warcraft player. I'm not exactly sure what playing a mythical creature in a made up computer-based world has to do with the fact that I can effectively put someone in a bracing hold and choke them out in three seconds, but in his mind, they were irrevocably connected like Twinkies and Mountain Dew.

He spent the entire 360 minutes of work bragging about his level 76 orc paladin from the fantasy driven virtual world. I spent the majority of the time resisting the urge to beat him with a rolling pin, while creating fantasies of my own about shoving him through the gigantic oven that was set to a constant temperature of 432 degrees. (Why that number, I haven't the foggiest clue, I'm pretty sure the pizzas would have tasted just as vile if we cooked them at 435.)

What little time that was not filled with detailed, blow by blow accounts of his adventures of tapping keys on a keyboard to make one virtual thing kill other virtual things, was instead rife with a list of the porn he had watched.

That was Thursday afternoon. By the next shift, a Friday evening, I had just barely managed to get my facial tic and gag reflex under control.

Friday nights were always busy. After all, what better way is there than starting your weekend with heartburn?

Everyone and their relatives, living and dead, wanted a pizza that particular night. T(vowel)M spent his time usefully following my coworker, Kirsten, and me around the shop trying to engage us in conversations about whether or not we thought he would make a good knight in real life.

At one point, I was hurriedly cutting a line of about six or seven pizzas when, suddenly, I felt another human being's presence. No literally, the person was close enough that I could feel them exhaling on my cheek. T(vowel)M nearly died via a pizza cutter as I leaped away. T(vowel)M, being a few Brady's short of a Bunch, did not take my surprised and angry response of, "Ack! What were you doing!?" as a negative sign.

Instead, like a paladin armed with a pink foam pool noodle he charged onwards into conversational doom. At this point the movie *Transformers* had just come into theaters (yes I am that old, get over it). He started with his super smooth opening line, "Have you seen *Transformers*?" I sighed, and returned to work while saying, "Nope."

He smiled at this and leaned in even closer, "Do you WANT to see *Transformers*?"

I could see where this was going and so quickly looked for an escape. My only modes of getting out were through the drive-up window, which was locked, or through the ravenous throng of waiting customers blocking the front door. Seeing no viable retreat, I simply shrugged, "No, I don't."

Now, when a person says that they have no interest in doing/dancing around/seeing something, that, to me at least, does not mean affirmation. Which is why I'm sure when he leaned in closer and asked, "So... would you like to see Transformers with *ME*?" my facial expression was one informing him that he was a few emus short of a herd. After a pause, in which I hoped he'd take the hint, I finally said, "No."

I anticipated that this would squelch any further conversation, but then again, I forgot who I was talking to; a level 76 paladin. One does not become a level 76 paladin by giving up when the server crashes or when your special armor doesn't save your from a group of evil pixies armed with torches.

No, one must persevere, and persevere he did. Leaning in so close I could not have held a peanut butter and jelly sandwich between us he, in his most smooth seductive tone, squeaked out, "So... are you busy Friday night?"

It was at this point that I had had enough, "I have to attend the opening of my garage door that night!"

I then propelled my 18-year-old body off to the other end of the store at a speed, which would have given the Flash a run for his money. From that day, until the day he was fired for yelling at a customer who insulted his sense of honor, I made a special effort to find cardboard boxes and heating lamps far more interesting than conversations with him. A task that was easier than finding something expensive in Bill Gates' house.

Here are the morals of our story:

1. If you wish to ask someone of the opposite sex out, and your idea for a date turns out to be something they have no interest in, don't blindly charge ahead. This is a plan doomed for as much failure as trying to take on a semi-truck in a game of chicken in a Geo-Metro.

2. The cliché, "If at first you don't succeed, try again," does not really apply in the dating world, especially if your second and third tries are within 20 seconds of each other.

3. Don't crowd short blond girls; had those customers not been there as witnesses T(vowel)M could have ended up in a body cast for his continual violation of my personal space.

4. For the love of heaven and hell, never work at Little Caesar's Pizza.

7. MOTHER HEIFER

I dislike cows. Despite the fact that I don't eat them, I dislike cows as much as I imagine Slash dislikes reading "Family Circus." Now, before anyone gets totally distracted by the mental image of Slash reading about Billy's latest adventure that no one cares about, let me explain my animosity towards bovines.

I am from a large Scottish family, a vast majority of whom are country folk who live in quaint little towns, which could easily become the setting for a horror movie that goes straight to DVD. This means that I am related to a ton of farmers, overalls included, whose farms I have spent unwilling family vacation time at.

When I was eleven, my mother decided to take us to visit her cousin Bob.

It is important to understand that at age eleven we had recently moved from Atlanta, Georgia, to Idaho. I was already in culture shock; I went from mile long parking lots and monstrous skyscrapers to endless fields of green stuff and an actual blue sky over my head. I didn't know what to do with all that breathable air and the sight of road kill chickens.

While I was still in this fragile, horribly befuddled, state my mother decided we should take a road trip through Oregon, a journey that took us right by her cousin Bob's dairy farm.

If you have never been on a dairy farm before, it is a very humbling experience. You suddenly realize, as you look out over hundreds to thousands of head of cattle, that if the cows ever decide to revolt then the human race, as we know it, is hosed. Luckily, from what I understand, cows have the intelligence of a sober Paris Hilton, so we should be safe.

Spring was in the air, as was the unimaginable stench produced by grass digesting, ethanol producing, walking steaks.

Spring also meant that cousin Bob was about to add to his herd of cattle. If you don't know what I mean, ask your parents.

While my mom chatted pleasantly with the rest of Bob's family, Bob decided to take me out to check on the pregnant cows. One bovine was actually in labor when we entered the barn where the pregnant cows were penned, to the point where two little hooves were protruding out the cow's tush like an accurate rendition of the *Alien* movies.

I specifically remember my uncle Bob saying, "Good, I'm glad you get to see this!" as if watching a cow squeeze out another cow was like getting to see Iron Maiden in concert. Bob climbed into the pen and began to pull on the protruding hooves.

With trepidation, I watched Bob play tug-o-war with a cow's uterus. Once the calf was about half emerged, cousin Bob suddenly looked over at me, and said, "Hey, come on in here and help me. You should learn how to do this."

I have never been afraid of blood, guts and gore. I may not be a country girl, but getting dirt on my hands does not bother me. Keeping that in mind, I still had no desire to, "learn how to do this," anymore than I wanted to learn how to leap through flaming hoops wearing a swimsuit soaked in gasoline. Still, being a somewhat obedient child, I climbed in the pen and slogged through the unmentionable mud to help pull on the calf.

I gave the calf a light tug, the cow made a noise that I'm sure came straight from the mouth of Mephistopheles himself, and I found myself somewhere that was smellier than a pack of decomposing hotdogs being lit on fire. I couldn't breathe and I heard weird bird noises and I felt like someone had dropped a bag of rotten potatoes on me.

I quickly realized that the lights swimming in front of my face were the swinging fluorescent lights of the pen, the chirping birds were Bob's chortles, and the bag of potatoes on my chest, stomach and legs, was breathing.

I lifted my head out of the cow crap and mud and came face to face with the back leg of a calf. Apparently, just as I had come to "help," the cow had given one mighty push and thus ejected the calf like a placenta-covered cannonball, where it landed on me.

My arms were pinned to my sides, making self-extraction impossible, and it was obvious from the belly-laughs coming from Bob that he was about as useful to me right now as fifty pounds of cheese is to a person who is lactose intolerant.

My only option was to lie there in the filth as the cow began to clean the calf and cousin Bob collected himself. Eventually, I was rescued from my predicament by a still jovially laughing Bob.

I learned two juicy lessons from this experience:

1. Never trust a man wearing overalls and orange rubber rain boots.

2. Cows are evil vile creatures that deserve to be made into delicious steaks and eaten by other people.

8. I WAS LATE TO CLASS BECAUSE

This is the tale of how I managed to break a toe and get whiplash in one fell swoop without the involvement of a motor vehicle or dinosaur attack. Impossible you say? Oh ye of little faith.

During my freshman year in college I had a roommate who was a small, adorable, Pentecostal, blond, who had never been to a concert in which anything stronger than "darn" was uttered by the band. That year, however, she won two tickets to a rock concert at a local concert house. Being a well-seasoned concert go-er (and yes I realize this makes me sound like I was, at some point, covered in thyme and garlic) she took me with her.

The concert house where this particular band was playing at had a reputation, a reputation that usually involved ambulances and really expensive hospital bills. Therefore, I was a tad nervous about taking someone who had been raised in a small peaceful town the size of my high school into a place, which was most likely going to be more violent than a *Rambo* movie.

As we walked into the concert I heard a voice boom above my head like Zeus from Olympus, "Allison!?!?"

I suddenly found myself dangling about a foot and a half off the ground as I was unceremoniously hoisted up by my armpits. A former coworker of mine, Travis, had apparently been hired as a bouncer by the concert house, and with good reason.

If one were to mix a grizzly bear with the Terminator one would get Travis. Standing at just over six feet five inches tall, plastered in more art than contained in the Louvre and sporting more body hair than a gorilla with a hormone issue, Travis wasn't exactly the first in line to get a job at a daycare center. Travis was also a few fries short of a happy meal. In fact it is probably safe to say that he was missing the toy and drink as well.

Feet still dangling, my roommate gawking like she had just been slapped with a salmon, I found myself at eye level with Travis who said, "Oh, it is you," and promptly dropped me back onto the ground.

A little dazed I said some quick pleasantries and herded my, still gaping open-mouthed, roommate into the concert.

Inside, the concert was starting and, as is usual with rock concerts, a mixture of intoxicated persons and those just looking for a fight started a mosh pit. Having never been to a rock concert, my roommate wanted to be right up close to the stage, which put her dangerously close to the edge of the mosh pit.

I'm glad the band wasn't a particularly fantastic one, as I spent a majority of the concert nudging her away from the edge of the mosh pit. I felt like a bodyguard for a lemming as she almost suicidally bounced back towards the dangerous throng. I was successful in keeping her from the maelstrom of flying fists and sweaty thrashing bodies for a majority of the concert.

At one point, however, I was a bit preoccupied with trying to convince a man, whose whiskey breath could have felled a buffalo at twenty paces, that really he didn't want to give me a hug, and my roommate wandered towards the edge of the chaotic pit of doom. I turned just in time to see a 200-pound man get a running start to ram a 300-pound man who was standing directly in front of my roommate. I grabbed and threw her to one side in an act of truly dumb and probably unnecessary heroism.

The next thing I knew, I was drowning, or at least that's what I was able to surmise since every time I tried to take a breath I inhaled some form of liquid. It wasn't until later that I found out, from my roommate, that I had been lying on my back with the man on top of me and my face in some very sweaty, shirtless, man cleavage.

Just as I thought my pinned body was done for, the overweight man was lifted off me like a burlap sack filled with ketchup and tossed aside. I began to feel like I was flying, soaring upwards, towards what I thought was heaven. I started to wonder if I had survived all the calamities of life only to die due to 300 pounds of sweaty concert attendee being dropped on me like an anvil on the head of a cartoon character.

I was quickly roused from this thought as I was suddenly shaken back and forth as Travis' voice boomed, "Is she alive!?"

I tried to tell him that I was ok, that really I could go on and lead a happy productive life full of puppies and rainbows, but the only thing that came out was, "glubble."

Travis took this as a sign that the shaking was effective and actually medically useful as he continued while saying oh so helpful things like, "I think she's breathing!"

Eventually my roommate came out of shock enough to convince Travis that maybe he should just take me to the edge of the crowd and set me down there.

23

I'm sure that I got up and walked back to the car, but I don't really remember that part. I do, however, remember seeing fairies dancing in front of my eyes for the next several hours.

I took the longest shower in recorded human history that night and washed the clothes I was wearing with more detergent than I would normally use in nine loads of laundry before I felt even slightly clean.

I then spent the next several days trying to explain to professors why I was walking with a limp and couldn't actually crane my neck upwards to see the projected PowerPoint slides.

So what is the moral of the story?

1. Knowing the bouncer has some advantages. However, if the bouncer also thinks himself a purveyor of medical treatment, then those advantages disappear faster than beer at a Super Bowl party.

2. "I was crushed by a man with bigger boobs than Dolly Parton and then shaken by a giant," apparently isn't a credible reason for showing up late to class.

9. HANG UP AND DRIVE

At one point I lived in Nampa, Idaho, and no you should not feel uneducated if you have never heard of it. Voted at one time as, "The Armpit of the Nation," this little farming community turned slightly larger farming community is home to pretty much nothing.

As itty-bitty as it is, there is a surprising number of what the locals refer to as "traffic jams." Despite the fact that rush-hour in this town can often turn a 30 minute drive into a 31 minute drive, there were several times when I found myself impatiently tapping on my steering wheel and singing along to *Love is a Battlefield*.

Several mile-long car pileups there do not occur at go-home time like in most other areas of the country. Instead, they happen during the middle of the day and are normally caused by things like people joy riding down the road in their tractors, or rebellious cows loping their way lazily across the street or even the occasional person attempting to move a refrigerator across the main thoroughfare by sliding it on top of cardboard boxes.

I was once 45 minutes late to work because I got stuck behind a cattle-drive, then a tractor, and then a person who apparently was still trying to figure out what the long skinny pedal on the right was for. On another occasion I came in late and had to explain to my boss that I had been stuck behind a group of dancing clowns.

Obviously, traffic jams in this place were not often caused by accidents, unless they were particularly horrible in which case everyone felt the sudden urge to stop and stare at the accident for approximately the same amount of time it takes to boil a tanker truck full of water using a candle.

There was road construction constantly, but since I never actually saw road construction work being done, that rarely was the cause of driving delays. One was more likely to get stuck behind a motor home that had set the cruise control to a snappy 35 miles per hour than get snared in the morning traffic.

There was one particular event, however, which dwarfed all of my absurd experiences driving combined.

I was driving home, blissfully ignorant as I sang loudly and out of tune to my radio, and came upon a line of cars that literally stretched back about a mile and a half. My mind immediately went to the most logical cause for a traffic jam like this; a dead cow.

The cars inched forward at the pace of diseased snails as car after car passed whatever the obstacle in the road was. As the time passed, and those of us trapped in our vehicles barely moved, I began to extrapolate on what the cause could be. Maybe someone had hijacked a tractor and decided to race away on the open road? Maybe someone was attempting to herd cats in front of us? As the time went on I began to believe more impossible scenarios, such as, maybe there is actual road construction being done!

After about half an hour of being caught in this moving death-trap it was finally my turn to pass the obstacle.

I'm sure the expression on my face of utter loss and confusion had been mirrored by the many people who had also run into the impediment that whirring forward in front of me. Smack dab in the center of the lane was a little old lady, grandma-fro included, riding what looked to be one of those handicapped scooters that one might get at Wal-Mart. Not only was she driving about three feet from a perfectly available sidewalk, but she was utterly ignoring the cars piling up behind her as she animatedly talked on her cell phone's headset.

Buzzing along at a practically racing three miles per hour this lady taught me a couple of very important lessons:

1. If you ignore problems, even ones the size of Mac trucks, sometimes they will just veer around you, leaving you untouched. Of course, if you are less lucky, then you might find yourself a permanent part of the Mac truck's front grill.

2. Even the smallest person can make a difference; in this case a single tiny little old woman turned my pleasant 15-minute drive into an hour-long nightmare.

10. LURKING DANGER

I have mostly had a good relationship with animals throughout my life. True, I have been chased by a turkey, bitten by a horse and sneezed on by a llama, but by and large the animal kingdom and I have had peaceful relations and very few border wars.

I'm normally fine snuggling up with an animal, assuming it has fur, has been bathed semi-regularly, doesn't inflict injury for fun and/or doesn't attempt to release any form of bodily fluid on my face. For the most part one could pretty much place me in that forest scene in *Snow White*, aside from horrid dress and a vibrato wide enough to drive a truck through, and I would be ok.

This all changed with Lord Byron. Lord Byron was the cat of a professor who let me, quite frequently, stay in her house while I was working in town over the summer. I also often pet-sat while she was gone.

Lord Byron weighed about as much as a pregnant killer whale and was not so much a cat, as a bowling ball with fur, legs and eyes. This kitty often had problems with not rubbing his belly on the ground when he walked, and often would give up on movement altogether and just flop down to merely roll across the floor.

Lord Byron also had a couple slight mental defects. One was that he had the worst separation anxiety in the world. He needed to be the center of the universe at all times, and considering his substantial size, that wasn't hard.

He also had the teensy weensy, hardly noticeable, habit of peeing on beds. He would not urinate indoors anywhere else, just on beds. Due to this fact he had a shock collar installed to keep him out of the professor's bedroom, and all other bedroom doors were also closed to him.

This only multiplied his desire to be around someone when they were locked away out of reach. Byron would sit outside a closed bedroom door for hours repeating the same routine of yowling in a tone comparable to someone beating a bagpipe next to a microphone that was having constant feedback issues, then scratching at the door, and then there would be silence.

The silence was misleading, a calm moment before the terror that Byron's next actions would always bring. One would feel relieved that Byron had lost interest, but then one would hear a rhythmic thudding noise.

The noise would grow, like a train laden with the entire cast of *Desperate Housewives*, spreading terror on the inhabitants of the room behind the closed door. Then, suddenly, "BOOM!" The walls would shake as the door sounded like it was about to come off its hinges. Lord Byron, in all of his kitty might, would get a running start and full on crash into the door like a cannon ball.

Byron always felt the need to do this at approximately three in the morning. As a result, I had multiple times in which I woke up believing I was in the middle of the Civil War.

Failing to rouse an immediate response from me, Byron would eventually wind down after an hour or so of repeatedly throwing his sizeable bulk against the door. This, however, was only a short reprieve, for somewhere, out in the rest of the house Byron was perched, waiting, and watching for a person to emerge.

In the morning I would blindly stumble from my room to get on with my morning. This newly awakened state made me easy prey for a needy kitty. At any time, from anywhere, Byron could spring. I would suddenly find my ankle bludgeoned from underneath a chair, or the back of my knee smacked from coffee table, he once even attempted to pounce on my face from atop the fridge.

For the most part, however, I was able to avoid most of Lord Byron's more serious attacks. I deftly dove and ducked to avoid the penalties in our furry game of dodgeball. Byron, however, was keeping score, and he got his revenge for my avoiding him tenfold.

One day, I was performing my normal morning routine of ridding myself of the previous day's adventures under a pipe driven waterfall. I was just about to start washing my hair when suddenly the shower curtain moved. This little movement was my only and last warning. Suddenly the shower curtain was flung back from the wall and something big and black was sitting in the shower with me.

I'm not entirely sure how Byron's tiny little mind thought this was going to turn out. I'm relatively sure his thought process was something along the lines of, "I will defeat the evil barrier keeping me from the human, then the human will pet me, and I will win."

It was only after Byron jumped into the shower with me did he realize, "Wait, this is wet, I don't like being wet."

There was a moment of shock between both parties, then, a maelstrom of activity only paralleled by a group of kindergarteners being given several shots of espresso and water guns. There was flailing as Byron's solution to being wet was to reach higher ground, in this case me.

The resulting tussle ended, after about 30 seconds of useless random movements from both parties, as Byron was ejected from the shower like a shot put. Both kitty and human remained traumatized for days afterwards.

The morals that we should gain from these stories:

1. Some animals need medication for their personality disorders.

2. Stay physically fit. You never know when you have to have the ability to hoist and throw thirty-five pounds of fur, claws and cat food.

3. Always, always, always, always check the bathroom door to make sure it is closed when you go to take a shower. Sure, one time it might be just your run of the mill psychopath who decides to invade your private time, but the next time it could be cat with dandruff that is roughly the size of William Shatner's ego.

11. WHERE'S MY CAPE?

College is a time of self-discovery, and what I discovered during college about myself is that I have a superpower. No, I can't fly, shoot laser beams out of various orifices or turn random objects into cottage cheese at will. My superpower is my ability to kill or move spiders without fear.

You may not believe this is a superpower, but considering my own personal experiences I would maintain that it is indeed a power at least greater than of Aquaman's. My sophomore year in college I actually had people, men included, who saved my phone number simply so they could call me to come and get rid of spiders for them.

My junior year of college one of my roommates, Shayna, was a girl about six feet tall and a thrower on the track team. Shayna once lifted me a foot and a half off the ground just to see if she could, and could probably actually throw someone as far as she trusted them. Shayna was the person in the dark alley you did not want to meet.

That year there were four girls living in apartment built for one and half, our bathroom was the size of a linen closet. Therefore, moving in meant that we had the chaos of four people's stuff in a very small living room/kitchen as we attempted to find places for all of it. It was like trying to fit a sperm whale in a soda can. At one point Shayna moved a trash can to find it a home and out from behind it skittered a spider the size of Robin Williams' current career.

I never actually saw Shayna move, but I did feel the whirlwind as she whooshed past me, clearing tables, boxes and other roommates. She finally landed on top of the sofa, where she proceeded to, and in the most adult manner, jump up and down on the sofa squealing, "Kill it! Kill it!"

Only after I swooped in and squished the spider and then stepped on the buggy corpse about ten times did she actually come down from the sofa. Hands on hips, just as my superhero predecessors before me, I then had the opportunity to say, "What the hell was that?"

When I pointed out that, had the spider somehow been able to chase her with it's tiny tenth of an inch long legs across the room, then undoubtedly it wouldn't have been able to crawl up the sofa and reach her, she gave me a look that I can only imagine coming from an Amish person who was just told that God would approve of zippers. She spent the rest of the day cautiously moving objects and having me come to kill any unwanted pieces of lint daring to look like spiders.

Another friend of mine, Amanda, is, despite her rather small size, the toughest girl that I have ever met. Amanda holds records and titles for things like weightlifting and alligator wrestling. Well, maybe not the second one, but she could if she so desired. This tiny little blond bombshell is the closest this earth will see in looks and talents to Wonder Woman, I swear.

This is the same girl that I found flicking bugs off a second story balcony only to receive the explanation that she wasn't killing them she was just "sending them on a joyride."

I was sitting next to this power-house during one of our classes that we shared and I noticed she was staring at a notebook, which was propped up on her knee. As she continued to read I noticed a spider crawling up her leg, a fact that I thought she was aware of. So calmly I said, "Hey, there's a spider on your leg."

There was a brief second in which she looked down at her leg. She blinked a couple of times, then there was an explosion. Amanda's eyes grew to the size of a weatherman's toupee as she levitated about two feet off the ground, taking the desk, all of her books and the entire class' attention with her. Like in a cartoon, she seemed to hang there for a second before shifting backwards about a foot and a half.

When she returned to earth, the spider was still there. She flailed in a manner which would make a windmill proud until I reached over and swatted it. From then on, if I saw a spider near Amanda in any way shape or form, my plan was to strike first with Flash-like speed, explain the presence of the eight-legged invader later.

Now, I don't consider myself a totally fearless person; I avoid clowns, sour milk and Paris Hilton just as much as the next person. I can understand why someone might have some trepidations about poisonous spiders or even those spiders from Africa that are the size of your head. Tiny little brown harmless spiders, though?

Come on, are we really afraid that these tiny little critters are going to suddenly, after who knows how many thousands of years of existence they have had, revolt and lead a spider revolution to destroy the human race? Well, lucky for humanity, if they did there would be a handful of us ready to pick up copies of Ayn Rand's *Anthem* and start squishing.

What lessons can be learned from this experience?

1. No matter how strong someone is, there is something that is their heeby-jeeby Kryptonite.

2. Embrace your superpower. It may not save someone from a burning building, but it might save someone from being trapped in a bathroom for four hours.

12. I'LL SEE YOUR QUIXOTIC LOOK AND RAISE YOU AN EYEBROW

To date, I have owned a whopping four cars total in my lifetime. And until my most recent addition, each one of them has been a huge gallomping Buick.

No, I really do not enjoy driving around a walk-in refrigerator on wheels that is harder to park than docking the Titanic in a jet-ski bay. The fact is, that bulky and unattractive as they are, they have a tendency to last.

I think, much like The Pyramids of Giza, Shakespeare's plays and Sean Connery's career, the Buick will prove to be a part of our civilization that others can look back on in wonder; a car that guzzles more gas than a fleet of tanker trucks lit on fire that could go from zero to 70 mph in about two hours.

The Buick's main appeals to me were two-fold. The first was that, like an armored Bengal tiger, nothing could touch it. On the road I was probably the safest motorist alive; namely because if I got into a head on collision with anyone, my car would get only a few chips in the paint and their car would end up looking like lemurs drove steamrollers over it.

The second and most important factor, was that Buicks last forever and so I could buy an old one super cheap. Because it was American made, I could also normally fix most little issues for next to nothing.

I have not only had three Buicks, but I managed to own those three in the space of three months. Now, one might ask, if Buicks are so Arnold Schwarzenegger tough, why on earth did I need three in the space of three months?

To truly explain this, I must work backwards. The car I presently own is a 1991 Toyota Camry. For those who don't speak cars, this means that I own a gutless piece of machinery, which has an annoying dinging noise for absolutely everything a driver could possibly do. Even this puttering little piece of tin-foil is better than the trio of Buicks.

The last one I owned was a 1987 Buick Park Avenue, which is like owning the car equivalent of the Da Vinci Code; someone, somewhere knows how to reconstruct this thing, but because it is an exceptionally rare piece of machinery and metal, I'm not sure that anyone short of Albert Einstein working with Henry Ford could possibly fix it.

Geri, which is short for Geriatric, was the quintessential luxury car of the 1980's, which means that it had four ashtrays and no cup holders. Underneath her creamy tan coat of paint sat a fuel system, which, until I bought it, held a fuel filter that had never been traded out by its ancient 92-year-old driver who had owned the car since its factory birth.

How did I come by Geri? Well the owner had had his license revoked for the "silly" reason that he was blind. He did not see what the big deal was, but being a law-abiding citizen, and after griping for two years, he decided to sell off his old and faithful car.

Geri was a good car, except for some minor flaws. For instance, because of all the crud in the fuel system, anytime you brought the car to a halt, you had a 50/50 chance of the engine cutting out on you. I got really, really good at throwing the car in park, switching the keys down to the off position, then starting the car again. I actually had friends who said that I needed to be timed to see if I could get a car-restarting world record.

Thanks to the engineers of the 1980's, Geri was built with some of the earliest button operated electric locks. Be jealous. In merit to Geri's advanced age, one could spend five minutes attempting to get the car to lock because the back door locks frequently jammed and no amount of button pushing, forcing the locks down or kicking the door in frustration could actually do anything to secure them.

Geri had hazard lights, but the totally rad plastic mechanism that was installed to turn off the hazard lights had broken. So one could turn on the hazard lights, but it required a hammer, needle nosed pliers and approximately twice as much time as it takes to make double fudge brownies to turn them off again.

Geri served me well, like a butler with legs of greatly differing size, for over a year. Then came the fateful day I moved from Nampa, Idaho to Spokane, Washington. I got 10 miles outside of Spokane and suddenly Geri began making a noise that sounded like a mouse stuck in the boot of a Russian whirling dervish dancer.

I stepped on the gas pedal to increase to interstate speeds, only to be greeted with an RPM meter that shot up into the danger zone, and a shuddering car that could only wheeze on at a speed that could have been beaten by a go-cart powered by an eggbeater.

34

Limping into Spokane, I reached a mechanic who took a look at my engine and promptly informed me that my car was like a 400-pound man who had eaten nothing but hot-dogs and steak his entire life.

"You're car's like a heart attack waiting to happen, I mean it could explode at any moment."

"What do you mean by explode?"

The mechanic looked at me and then made some whirling hand motions while making the onomonopia noise of, "Kaboom!"

I staggered Geri to the nearest junkyard and sold her for a couple hundred bucks.

Because the junkyard was off of the interstate I had to put the car's hazard lights on so that no one would crash into me as I drove at 35 miles an hour in a 65 mile an hour zone. I got there, the hazard lights going blinkablinkablinka, parked, blinkablinkablinka, sold the car and got my money, blinkablinkablinka, and then watched as the lady came to get the keys from me.

"Umm... ma'am can you turn off the hazard lights?"

I'm not proud to say that, with the check in my hand, I made a break for it and left the staff of that junkyard to figure out the mysteries of disconnecting the switch from the lights, but I did.

The car I had before Geri was a 1996 Buick Regal that I had dubbed Rigor Mortis. Rigor was, in literary terms, the maroon cousin of The Great White Whale from *Moby Dick*. Now, Rigor was not just any Buick Regal, it was the Olympic Edition Buick Regal. This basically meant that it had the Olympic rings embossed, stitched or otherwise attached to every available surface; hubcaps, seat cushions and interior of the glove box included. I think if Rigor had actually participated in the Olympics it would have competed in curling; namely because no one watches it and no one fully understands it.

I had owned Rigor for about two and a half months, when I started to notice something rather odd. If I turned the car on and immediately put it into reverse, or heaven forbid drive, then I could rev the engine until trees turned into jam but I would remain sitting there doing nothing more than making a lot of really annoying noises.

If I gave Rigor about five minutes to warm up then I could throw it into reverse and rapidly find myself in third gear drive, which for an automatic is impressive. Now, this was no problem if I needed to get somewhere just slightly faster than a group of constipated cattle. However, Rigor would have failed miserably if I had needed to suddenly follow someone in a high-speed pursuit for stealing my socks.

I soon, through asking mechanically oriented people I know, found out that this was a problem with my transmission. This had been my second guess behind evil fairies living in my wheel well. Apparently a previous owner had done something to the transmission, like beat it with a baseball bat or told it "Yo Mama" jokes until it gave out in nervous exhaustion.

Repairing the transmission was going to cost about three times what I had paid for Rigor originally. This meant that as soon as the transmission gave out I would be the proud owner of the world's heaviest paperweight.

By complete luck I ran into the man who wished to get rid of Geri and persuaded him to trade cars with me. Since he couldn't drive whatever he had anyways, and mine had one of those newfangled CD players, he agreed to the swap.

Now, one might inquire as to what made me go with the epically long-lived Rigor Mortis? Certainly no car could last less than two and a half months of driving time? Unfortunately, reader, if you made that assumption you would be more incorrect than spelling your own name wrong on the SATs.

Mortimer, a 1994 Buick Regal, was every young adult's first dream car. If that dream involved smelling like old lady perfume, being able to reach 43 miles an hour only if dropped from a bomber and seat cushions that matched the maroon/brown exterior paint job, that is.

Fake wood paneling, a radio that featured both FM and AM radio stations if the winds were right and steering that made one feel like they were in a sailing vessel during a violent storm, Mortimer left all other cars that could be bought for next to nothing in the dust.

I bought Mortimer from a car dealership with the arrangement that I would pay the asking price for the vehicle if the dealership would send it to their mechanic to get a small electrical problem in the steering column fixed. They agreed to this, sent the car off, and gave my number to the mechanic.

The car was supposed to be finished in the shop that next Monday. I got a call from a mechanic, who sounded like he got great entertainment from watching the bug zapper on his porch at home, "Ms. Hawn? I'm sawry but dat car ain't gonna be done until Wednesday, k?" Knowing this was the way of mechanics I said, "Sure, just call me when it's done."

Wednesday rolled around and my phone rang, "Ms. Hawn? I'm sawry, but we found some doohickey that wasn't raht, so we's not gonna be done 'til Friday." I sighed and resigned myself to the knowledge that there was nothing I could do to make the process go any faster without using a chainsaw illegally.

Friday came, and I anxiously awaited a call informing me that I could finally come pick up my car. The call came as I was sitting with a group of friends. What they got to hear from my end went something along the lines of, "Yes, hello. Wait... what!? No... is that even possible!? Alright, I'll speak with the dealer."

As my friends watched on I contacted the dealer and then after waiting for a few minutes my friends were graced with this conversational nugget, "Hi, it's Allison Hawn... Yes I bought that Buick from you last week. Yes, the mechanic called me back. No, they hadn't finished it yet. Well, I don't think it will ever be finished. I don't think a car with a transmission that has recently been lit on fire is really drivable, that's why."

Somehow these mechanics, as in people who are trained to work on cars, managed to light the transmission in my car on fire. I spent the next few days postulating with my friends as to how this calamity could possibly have occurred.

Amanda suggested a blowtorch accident, Annie suggested that they had actually lit the entire car on fire and were just downplaying the damage and Caleb claimed that it was the work of Satan, while my theory was a birthday cake with candles accident. The truth is I will never know for sure, but what I do know is that I owned that car a grand total of seven days.

Owning three Buicks in three months has indeed taught me some important lessons.

1. Everything burns, even parts of car engines that are made almost entirely out of metal.

2. Just because someone is an "expert" in something doesn't mean that they will avoid a total disaster in their field. This lesson can also be learned from today's weather forecasters.

3. The only way to kill a Buick is via me owning it.

13. UZIS FOR EVERYONE!

Comparing my family's vacations to other families' vacations is kind of like trying to compare a herd of wombats stuffed in a hatbox to the Betty Crocker Cookbook. My family does not go on normal vacations. "Vacation time" never implies a cruise, resort or even an across country road trip in our bunch.

No, instead my family vacations have been spent visiting relatives in farm country, going on tours of underground caverns and getting the birds and the bees explained to me at Disneyland.

One of the more recent and interesting of these survival trips was somewhere my mom really wanted to go; a tactical gun training course. Not only was this a tactical defensive gun training course, this was a tactical defensive gun training course in the middle of the Nevada desert.

The four-day course included everything from firing a gun from the holster, to fixing your gun in a firefight, to how to stop a home intruder armed with a hand grenade.

Don't ask me why a home intruder, probably intent on stealing your earthly possessions, would be armed with a hand grenade. This was not a question I asked. In fact, I did not ask many questions in semi-fear of being shot.

We were required to wear our gun belts, guns and extra magazines at all times. This made peeing, as a female, almost impossible. Attempting to pee with all that equipment strapped to oneself is kind of like trying to use a hula-hoop made out of iron while not moving at all.

The training was indeed very professional. By the end of the course I could competently shoot a paper target, as long as my diminutive fingers could reach the trigger on the Glock that I was instructed to use.

The instructors even, after a couple days of training, had us go through a police style raid to shoot paper targets that looked more like actual human beings. The entire way through the instructors kept reminding me that if it was too disturbing to be shooting something so "lifelike," I could go do something else for a while.

I'm not sure what part of shooting paper targets in a shell of a house was supposed to be disturbing. Were there moral implications to shooting something propped up on sticks that I wasn't aware of? Was I depriving little paper targets of their mother or father with my wonton acts of violence?

Throughout the house simulation we were supposed to pick out innocent targets from baddies armed with everything from handguns to knives. At one point I turned a corner to see a guy holding a 1990's cell-phone. You know what I'm talking about, the ones that were roughly the size of a cinder block and weighed about as much as 1972 Mustang, but with far less class?

After a brief pause, I shot the picture. The dismayed instructor yelled, "You haven't shot a single innocent guy so far, why did you shoot this one, you even took your time before shooting him!?"

My only response was to point to the cell-phone and say, "He could have bashed my head in with that faster than the guy over there with the grenade could have killed me." The instructor did not question any of my further decisions.

This particular camp was run by an enterprising scientologist, who looked quite a bit like Tom Selleck. This meant that throughout the camp we were exposed to multiple lectures/videos on how America is going straight to Hell in a flaming flowerpot. Now, before I explain this next bit, let me explain to you my views of gun-control. I believe in the right to bear arms.

This does not mean that I think everyone should be allowed to pack whatever weapon they wish. Can the average Joe/Jill own a handgun for home or self-defense? With the correct training and a lack of criminal record, sure! Should Joe/Jill own a missile launcher? Only in the event of a zombie apocalypse or if *Jurassic Park* actually became real, otherwise, hell no!

The group this camp was run by saw just about any form of gun control as tyrannical oppression. Lawmakers and legislators were likened to mass murderers like Mao and Stalin. Videos were shown almost constantly about how gun control, any gun control, would basically lead to the downfall of the United States as we know it!

There was even a video shown in which a father was proudly stating that he was already training his two-year-old son how to shoot a .44 Magnum.

Having at one time lived in Idaho, I have seen fully-grown adults attempt to shoot a .44 Magnum and crack themselves in the forehead when it kicked back on them. I think that kid has as much chance of successfully firing that gun as my rat, Smeraldina, had of running for president. Not to mention, what kind of parent gives a two-year-old that kind of firepower? Can you imagine trying to put that kid to bed? You'd need the police in full riot gear!

There was many a time that I wanted to say, "But... wait, what?" but since everyone in the camp was required to be armed 24/7 I pretty much kept my mouth shut and, therefore, lead free.

This was incredibly difficult, namely because my mind to mouth filter has holes in it that one could drive a military Hummer through, and because as the days wore on I grew more and more exhausted, particularly by seeing camo everywhere I went.

This is just my own personal bent, but I do have to ask what the purpose of pink camouflage print is? I understand green and blue, though not in the middle of the desert, but pink? Where are you going to blend in cupcake, the Barbie aisle at Wal-Mart?

I think my favorite quote of the several day, no cell-phone reception, span came from a conversation I happened to overhear. I was plopped down eating my lunch at a table, which was next to a group of four rather burly men. You know what kind of men I mean, the ones that wear 1970's flannel plaid to attend their sister's weddings, with beards that could probably stop a rifle round.

They were all talking about what they were going to use their guns to protect. One man vehemently said, "I'm gonna protect my family!"

Another chimed in even more forcefully, "I'm gonna protect my house!!"

The next guy, in a tone that was dead serious and even more booming said, "I'm gonna use my gun to protect the Lord Jesus Christ!!!"

I was in utter shock, which probably saved my life, because if I hadn't been I probably would have laughed myself into being filled with enough lead to be used as a pencil. I sat there attempting to figure out how one might protect Jesus, who is not really on this earth anymore physically, with a gun?

Was this man's plan to go back in time and shoot Judas? I can just picture this plaid flannel shirted, lumberjack look-alike, individual saying, "No, no, step back Jesus, those Romans have got 20 men, but I've got 120 rounds!"

What was this guy going to do if someone made a bad comment about Jesus, shoot them!? I'm pretty sure Jesus, who was, aside from the money changers in the temple incident, a really peaceful guy, would not exactly be patting this guy on the back and saying, "Here's another clip, and the Holy Spirit has a few fresh magazines for you too."

All I know, is this is why I like to plan my own vacations.

What scrapings of intelligence can be gathered from the peeling paint of my encounters?

1. The ability to keep one's mouth shut is a survival skill second to none.

2. Never trust the phrase, "Hey, I think this place in Nevada will be a great opportunity for you." Think about the industries run out of Nevada. The pleasant options are few and far between.

3. The sight of enough non-military camo can cause brain damage.

14. THAT LEARNIN' DONE ME SOME GOOD

One of my more interesting jobs was working for a conferences and events center. What did I do there? Everything. I did lighting, customer service, sewing 3 stories off the floor, etc.

We ran several high school and college graduations in my time at this particular center, ranging in attendance from 1,500 people to 40-ish people. One of our smaller graduations was for six graduates and was held in one of our smaller rooms.

Because, we were expecting fewer attendees than to an enema party, I was the only one working this event. This meant that I was the sound person, lighting person, security, customer service and the person who unclogs the toilet all wrapped up into one 5'3" frame full of determination, knowledge and insanity.

This particular graduation had a grand total of six graduates, at least three of whom had their children either present at the graduation or developing from a zygote at the ceremony.

I watched as the 30 or 40 people filed in. There were brightly colored Hawaiian shirt wearing grandparents, middle-aged men wearing Budweiser t-shirts that were more hole than shirt and the scariest transvestite I have seen in my life, complete with hairy arms and face, slingback heels, the wrong shade of lipstick and a shorter skirt than someone could ever convince me to wear. This was a classy, classy bunch.

You know how there is that one moment, that single instance, where you know something is going to go terribly, horribly, horrendously wrong? It's that slight lean in the first bookcase in a row of bookcases, the small child looking earnestly at a priceless vase, the creepy guy that you accidentally make eye contact with as you are walking to work.

In this case my sign of impending doom came when the principal of the graduating class stood and watched me as I set up a metal folding table. She stared on as I pulled the legs solidly from their folded position, she gazed upon me as I righted the table and even followed me as I set it where she requested it, only to then ask, "Is there any way that we could make that table shorter?"

Anyone who has ever held a job in their lives knows that there are comments one would love to make to a client, but that if you ever did the skies would open and your boss, riding a flaming skeletal horse, would descend and fire your ass faster than a vegetable oil covered monkey can be slid down a play pen slide.

What I wanted to say was, "Not unless you have a hacksaw or you have a way to magically drill holes in the floor."

What I actually said was, "Umm... I'm afraid that this table is constructed in such a way that it is not adjustable."

She gave me a disappointed glance and walked away shaking her head.

The festivities eventually got under way. The set-up was so incredibly simple that a blind llama on crack could have done it. Crowd control, on the other hand, was much less straightforward. As the graduating class marched down the tiny center aisle, a small mohawked child, who apparently had lost his vertical hold on reality, began to run around the entire ceremony screaming at the top of his 4 or 5 year old lungs.

I stood by aghast as the child proceeded to run a figure-eight around the two sections of seating in the small auditorium continuing his loud war-cry. Not a single person batted an eyelash or attempted to stop his activities. The only reaction his actions garnered was that about every sixth lap one of his lame-ass parents would give him a Skittle as he passed.

This made about as much sense to me as giving a potential bank robber the blueprints and security codes to every bank in the city. Not only was this rewarding the kid's bad behavior, but it was giving him more energy to compete with the graduating class speaker, who, despite the microphone's obvious presence on the podium, opted instead to yell his entire speech.

Eventually I got the parents' attention and got them to quiet their small hellion. I shouldn't have bothered. The next thing I knew someone's phone went off at a volume that I swear could have been heard in a mosh-pit at a Disturbed concert. I watched as, accompanied by her own theme music, a woman got up and left the room, her phone still ringing. She then proceeded to stand outside the open door and yell into her phone with enough force to make the doors rattle.

It was as I was ushering her out of the building at arm's length, she had some scary looking long nails, I noticed that the elevator of the two-story building, seemed to be running. This was odd, because the entire graduation was housed on one floor. Therefore, no one should have been in the elevator.

I waited by the doors to the elevator as it came down from the second floor. The doors opened, and there stood two women, probably in their mid-40's. I was bemused into silence, like a cow looks at and incoming out of control hippie bus, just long enough for the doors to close again and the elevator to once again go up to the second floor. This pattern continued, with my attempts to get them off the elevator increasing in intensity.

If you have never had the experience of telling middle-aged women to stop joy-riding in an elevator or you will have to call security, then let me tell you, there are few things in life that will test your immediate sanity more.

I'm not sure what they were thinking. Maybe they believed that if they hit the up button enough the elevator would transfer them to a secret third floor or that it would magically produce a mountain of chocolate? I don't know and I honestly do not want to know.

By this point, the small mohawked child had resumed his previous activity, except with his short break of sitting on a chair, he seemed to have gathered even more of his magical banshee-like abilities. Flabbergasted, I plopped myself down on a chair and listened to the recessional as the graduating class walked and waddled towards the back of the room.

So what flower petals of knowledge can be viciously plucked from the stem of this experience?

1. Just because someone is employed by a school does not actually mean that they are intelligent.

2. The headaches caused by a small, screaming child can eventually be squelched with a glass of wine after work.

3. The approximate amount of two story elevator rides one can take in five minutes is around seventeen.

15. ONE, TWO, PLATYPUS, HUT!

I have tried for years to find a way to illustrate my rather odd body type. I'm short, broad shouldered and have more muscle overlaying my bones than society normally deems appropriate for a young woman.

I'm very obviously female though, thanks to some curves that are more dramatic than a high school rendition of a Shakespearean play.

Society can bite me, by the way. I may not be thinner than a wafer cookie, but I can carry my own damn groceries and have yet to need help moving furniture around my apartment.

After various attempts, the use of a thesaurus and a national survey study, I have determined that the only way to describe myself is as a curvy mini-fridge.

The only reason I try to give the reader a mental image of myself is to explain why I was placed as a lineman on my college intramural female football team, The Bruisers.

Sure, the sign-up sheets read "flag-football," implying that the players would only be making contact that was fluffier than the touch of a cloud. The reality, however, was that women's football on our campus was more violent than a reenactment of World War II produced by lemmings and a hungry pride of lions.

With no helmets or body padding of any kind, six or seven teams of determined women would crash into each other every weekend like the other team had kidnapped Ryan Reynolds and were holding him captive all to themselves. I once wore a tank-top to work during football season and I was repeatedly asked why only my sleeves were tie-dyed.

Our team was one of the most fearsome, fearless and driven groups of women that the campus had ever seen. We came from all parts of campus, track athletes, elementary education majors, track athletes, girls who took kickboxing, theater girls, track athletes and someone's cousin that was drafted at the last second. What can I say? I came from a small campus so the track team was basically our player pool.

The team was comprised of type A, ambitious, athletic bitches who locked our hearts in steel boxes before every game so that we

45

would feel no remorse when we watered the grass with the blood of our opponents.

Our coaches, most of whom played football back in high school, trained us how to run complicated plays with names like, "School Yard," "Banana Left," "Warrior Princess," and "Platypus."

We would enter the field, smiling sadistically, and watch as the opposing teams that had bonded together over silly values like friendship, hope, and being in the same chemistry class would quake. We steamrolled over our opponents like an aircraft carrier plows over a rowboat manned by limbless shrews, and we loved it.

One weekend we showed up to play our selected opponents, only to find that only three members of the opposing team had actually shown up.

Sad that our need for blood was not going to be filled that weekend The Bruisers grumbled in estrogenic unison.

Then, one of our coaches had an idea: Why not have the coaches, male referees and the three members of the opposing team brave enough to show up, play a just-for-fun game against us?

We heartily agreed. What next occurred was the most awkward game of football in the history of the sport.

Too late the guys realized some important details. For instance, the flags that we wore around our waists draped the tags one was supposed to grab and pull off around our butts and lady parts. This meant that a majority of the game was spent with the guys doing their very best to grab flags without also grabbing something else that would get them pile driven into the ground by our entire team.

At one point my friend Annie, who is a long-legged, triple jumping track athlete, had possession of the ball and began running for a touchdown. In close pursuit was our coach Dan, who was a distance runner.

If you have ever watched a parent attempt to chase after an escaping toddler, then you know what I mean when I say "the waddle." For those who have never seen this phenomenon, basically imagine yourself trying to catch a herd of ducklings wearing spiked cleats. The wide-legged gate that Dan threw out as he attempted to chase Annie without getting a handful of butt was hilarious but ineffective. We scored, thanks to gentlemanly behavior.

Not all of our plays were as effective, however. At one point one of my fellow linemen, Amanda, found herself facing off against Sooki. Sooki was basically built like a brick wall backed by thirteen semi-trucks and an army of polar bears.

Amanda crouched low, waiting for the call of "hike!" Finally the play was called and the ball was thrown back. Amanda exploded forward with the strength and power of a million steroid enhanced gazelles, only to smack directly into Sooki's stomach and ricochet back down to earth.

Sooki looked down at Amanda with an expression like he had just knocked his mother's favorite vase down the stairs, and now he wasn't sure if he should attempt to pick up the pieces and glue them back together, or if he should just leave it alone and see if it magically repaired itself.

The Bruisers suffered our first defeat of the season, but the game was very close. Though, if we were counting the score of bruises inflicted, I think we would have won. Despite our non-record-harming loss, that was the best game we had all season.

Of course there are some important takeaway messages from our adventures:

1. Just because you sign up for a "limited contact" sport doesn't mean that there won't be opponents who believe limited means only 98.7% bodily contact.

2. In sports, if you can't score by brute force, then score with pure awkwardness.

3. Eventually, the extremely conservative guy who grabbed your tush will stop blushing every time he sees you. However, this won't happen until approximately the graduation ceremony as you exit college.

16. I'LL JUST LIVE IN A CARDBOARD BOX, THANKS THOUGH

My first job after completing my undergraduate degree was a two year placement in Spokane, Washington with a non-profit organization working with street youth.

This mentally affirming job unfortunately was less positive in the pay scale. This meant that, between moving, just getting out of and paying for a private university education, I was on a budget tighter than Richard Simmons' spandex.

I had made a list of appointments of apartments to look at before I arrived in Spokane, and set out to find a livable space that wouldn't cost more than buying enough gum to keep a softball team happy for a year.

The first two places I toured were managed by the same realty company. The realty group sounded upscale and respectable when I first contacted them. Their very name sounded like even their furniture was used to wearing a full suit and tie.

Excited to find a new place, I went to meet up with their representative at the first place they told me about. I suddenly found myself greeted by a woman wearing a polyester shirt, with a pattern that should have died in the 1980's, and loafers.

I introduced myself as I followed the shuffling realtor towards the first place.

The realtor opened the door to the apartment and part of the doorway fell with a thud onto the deepest poop-brown shag carpet I had ever seen. The realtor, not even fazed by the piece of wood that nearly hit her in the head, flipped on the light and the sounds of scurrying little legs and paws could be heard.

Already I could tell that this was not the place for me. I don't mind having roommates, but having around 3,000 of them living in various places you might step or keep food is not as desirable.

The realtor pressed on, despite my protestations, and lead me into a bedroom that looked like it had last been cleaned when Nixon was saying, "I am not a crook," on national live television. Doing everything she could to try and sell me on this apartment, she led me towards a door in the back bedroom while proclaiming, "The room has a walk-in closet."

She wasn't lying. The room did have a rather large walk-in closet. This fact would have been far more impressive if there wasn't a sewage tank installed in the middle of it. It's true one could store lots of clothes in there, but unless you were made entirely from Silly Putty and could squeeze past the sewage tank, you could not reach them, not to mention the implications of storing one's clothes right next to the sewage tank that serviced the entire apartment building.

The realtor was shocked when I turned down her offer.

I agreed to go see the other apartment that she had to offer simply because I thought that there was no way on this pollutant-filled planet the other place could be any worse.

The next place I was shown was a basement apartment, which sounded just dandy to me. Basement apartment usually translates into small, but affordable and easy to keep cool living space. In this case it meant something more along the lines of, "You will be raped and murdered down here and no one will find the body for years."

As we drove towards this house where the apartment was, I began to relax. I watched as neatly cut lawns and cute little front gates whizzed past us in the car like some kind of homage to the 1950's dream-life. Every little house on the street was well-maintained and healthy looking, except one.

We then pulled up in front of a house that looked like it had possibly been used as batting practice for the Jolly Green Giant.

The paint was peeling off in flakes the size of my hand, it appeared to me that large jungle game could be hiding in the lawn and the house was missing large chunks that had all been covered with duct tape and, in one spot, a confederate flag.

The ever-determined realtor herded me to a back door which she kicked open, exposing a staircase that looked like it led into the set of an Alfred Hitchcock film. Since I didn't offer to go first, she plodded on down the stairs, each one making a non-reassuring bending creak as she put her weight on it. At one point one of the stairs made a noise like the jaws of an alligator slamming shut on some small helpless bird.

"Oh, well, we'll get that stair fixed soon," she said perkily as she instructed me not to step on the board which had just snapped.

The basement was multi-purpose. It not only housed the apartment, but it was extra storage for the other tenants who lived in the house. As I looked around I found myself facing two doors.

49

"Umm... Is there another apartment down here?"

"Nope! One of those is the door to your apartment, the other is the door to your bathroom!" She said this with such enthusiasm that I actually thought she believed this to be a perk.

Utterly ignoring my looks of disdain she began talking about the living situation.

"So here's the bathroom."

She unlocked a small linen closet with a toilet and a shower that looked comfortable only for Smurfs. This meant that to go to the bathroom, I would have to leave my apartment, go around the corner and unlock another door, all the while making sure I had my key because it was possible to lock oneself into the bathroom.

"Now, let me get the lights on."

I watched in astonishment as she reached, not inside the bathroom where one might guess a light switch would hide, but to the outside wall about six inches from the door. So, basically, I could be showering, and one of the other tenants, who all had keys to the basement, could come down and flip the lights out on me.

I slammed my eyes shut hoping that this was some terrible nightmare, like the kind where I'm being chased by clowns on pogo sticks. When I reopened my eyes, the realtor had moved on to the actual apartment.

She opened a cheap plywood contraption that I'm not entirely sure could be classified as a door, and we stepped onto the oldest linoleum I had ever seen. I'm not sure what color it was originally, but at that time the entire floor was a deep murky brown.

The entire apartment's interior was not much bigger than the inside of a camper trailer, and it smelled far worse.

"And here's the heating units," she said effervescently looking down at some wall heaters that looked like they might crumble if someone touched them.

"And here's the fridge," she said reaching for the fridge door handle and yanking it open.

The scent that filled the room was worse than the smells produced after a Southern chili feed. She quickly slammed the door shut saying, "You know, we don't need to look in there."

And she was right. By the time she turned around I had found the exit and was using it.

As I was hastily departing, she handed me some applications and said, "If you want to rent either place, just call!" I stepped out into the sunlight, turned and saw one of my possible fellow tenants sitting on the front porch smoking what appeared to be crack. I looked back at the realtor, and said, "Yeah, I'll consider it."

I considered it all the way to the car, where I climbed in and left all of my considerations in a pile sitting just out of reach of the gate that was coming off of its hinges.

What nuggets of knowledge can be gleaned from the caverns of my experience?

1. If the first place the realtor shows you is terrible, and it's their "nicer" place, don't expect something livable from the next one. That's kind of like expecting the neighbor's psychotically happy black lab puppy not to tackle you with joy whenever you try to come over.

2. Come up with a plan of action to escape realtors who may attach themselves to you like a terrier on a pant leg. I don't care if your plan of retreat involves a gas mask, napalm and a helicopter. It may be worth it.

17. SCARING PEOPLE ONE TREE AT A TIME

I am an extreme problem solver in the sense that if I am faced with a quandary, I can spring into action with MacGyver-like abilities. However, I am not the type of woman who often pauses to think thoughts like, "What will this look like to neighbors/my family/random passersby/insane asylum directors?"

I have the proud distinction of once having turned the simple task of getting a coworker's nametag out of a tree into a first rate fiasco.

While I was working at the conference center, I had a coworker named Matt who was a sweet and smart enough guy, but he was also a bit impulsive. Basically, Matt is a Border Collie puppy. He is the kind of person that someone could say a phrase such as, "That's like forgetting to put on your pants," and Matt would respond with, "So, funny story..."

That day, Matt was given the task of running between two of our buildings to keep an eye on clients and report any needs to the main crew back at our building. Matt tends to turn boring activities into absolute swashbuckling adventures; he could happily play with a rubber band and a paperclip for hours.

In search of any form of entertainment on his walks between the buildings he decided to see if he could get his nametag to stick into the ground. Now, for those who have never attempted to get their work nametag to lodge itself in solid earth, Matt found that he had to get quite a bit of height for the nametag to break through the freshly manicured lawn and plant itself. He tried this several times with no success. Slightly miffed, he threw it even higher only to have it not return to earth.

Matt came into the office with a, "someone just kicked my kitten," kind of expression which, of course, garnered attention from everyone working in the office. We all then got our dose of bizarre for the day as he announced that his nametag was lost in a pine tree.

Unfortunately, Matt needed to keep running between buildings, and everyone else in the office was watching the guests we had in our main building (in case one decided to steal our giant statue that was in the shape of bacon), so I was elected to do the honors of getting his nametag out of the pine tree for him.

I gladly accepted my mission, namely because it sounded like a challenge, and I tend to accept challenges to my honor, even when there is nothing honor-threatening about them. My task was complicated by the fact that almost every door, including those to the prop storage, janitor's closet or woodshop, were blocked by too many customers that one could not shove past to get something useful. Therefore, I was restricted to what I could find in the office. My options, just to lend to how odd my job was, were a broom and foam prop bloody disembodied hand.

So, in the middle of summer, in a suit, I found myself beating a tree with a broom and a grotesque piece of stagecraft.

Now, our business bordered a local university that was at he height of its recruitment season. As I was in my own little reality of nametag recovery, I found myself becoming more and more aware of approaching voices. I turned just in time to find myself facing an audience of prospective university students on tour of the lovely campus.

I can't imagine what was going through these poor little students' minds. First they are coming to a college campus, which is scary enough on its ownsies, but now they are faced with a random woman beating the crap out of a pine tree.

Now, when I get nervous or realize that I am doing something socially unexplainable my stock reaction is to wave. It was exceedingly unfortunate then that the hand I chose to wave was also holding onto the prop foam limb.

I believe the proper term for what the entire group did in unison was, "skedaddled." As the tour guide whisked them away at a speed that could compete with a jetpack-clad cheetah, I found myself learning some important lessons.

1. If your coworker does something dumb, do not offer to try and fix the mistake. He can do that himself later.

2. Always check your hands before you wave to someone, particularly someone new.

3. If you ever have to explain to your boss why you were beating a tree out in front of his building, and you have a legitimate reason, then it may be time to start looking for a new job.

18. HERE IS WHERE YOU SHOULD NOT BE

I have had the opportunity in my lifetime to go and see pretty incredible places: I've hiked into Petra, stopped a pickpocket in Paris and learned why not to drink the water in Mexico.

In my adventures, I got the opportunity to go to Israel with my grandparents and a small group of interested people.

My Grandfather has been to the Middle East, particularly Israel, more times than Lindsay Lohan has been in the news for drunk driving. During his time there, he acquired a friend by the name of Zac, who was to be our guide while we were there.

If there were ever an evolutionary theory stating that man came from camels, Zac would have been the missing link. Pushing 70 years old, Zac had spent most of his life outdoors in the Israeli sun, proving to me once and for all that sunscreen was vital for me not looking like Yoda when I reached 50.

Zac knew everything about his native country; his family had lived there for, from what I could gather, a trillion years, and his knowledge was more expansive than one could find on Wikipedia.

Zac, due to his age, was also a little forgetful. He would frequently overlook that we were from a different country and would begin randomly speaking in one of many languages he knew. He would then gaze around with satisfaction at his own little speech, and see a small audience of faces that were more bemused than as if they had all just witnessed hippos dancing the tango to *Viva Las Vegas*.

Even when Zac's answers to our questions were in English, it was often harder to decipher what he meant than trying to get a secret message out of one's Alphabet Soup. Anytime anyone asked where we were, Zac would be super helpful and say, "Here is where we are."

If anyone wished to know how far we were from a particular destination, his blanket response was, "We are in the area." It was like trying to ask questions of an old male version of Sarah Palin.

At one point in our travels through Israel, Zac decided to take us up high in the hills so that we could see over his beloved country. We drove for over an hour, up through this winding hill and mountain path. As we got higher, the road became thinner and less professionally paved. Furthermore, there were several times when we had to stop so goats could cross the road in front of our struggling vehicle. For nearly an hour we saw no other human beings as we continued to wind our way up what was becoming a rather scarily narrow dirt road.

Eventually our vehicle came upon a tiny little town that looked like it may have already seen and somehow survived an alien robot invasion. As we all got out, we felt the concerned and bemused glances of pretty much the entire town. No matter where we went, people looked at us like we were dressed like Lady Gaga clones or running through the streets on fire in spandex unitards.

We ate lunch in a small shop. The owner and workers did not speak to us at all, they would only speak with Zac, all the while shooting furtive glances at us like we might all be carrying live rabid chipmunks on our persons. I chalked this up to the language barrier and happily ate my falafel.

A couple hours later we left the hills and returned to billboard and soda drinking, civilization. As we were continuing on our trip my grandfather turned to Zac and asked, "Zac, we haven't ever been up there before."

Zac smiled and got that faraway look in his eyes, the look that said he was reaching through the recesses and catacombs of his mind, "Yes, I would never take white people (his name for anyone American/Canadian/European) up there, last time they were up there, they got shot at..."

Zac was brought out of his revelry to the sight of several identical expressions of, "WHAT!?!?" Zac took a deep breath and said, "Ah, yes, you are all white... well lucky for you things have calmed down."

What lessons can be learned from this little escapade?

1. It really is worth one's while to dig through the obscured wording and the language barrier to find out exactly where one is in a foreign country.

2. When it matters most, remind your friendly tour guide what country you come from so he will remember where taking you might end with you being filled with bullets.

19. ONE BAD TRIP

I can happily say that a majority of allergies have passed me by in my life like bundle of gerbils being flung over the top of Wrigley Field. Granted with a smattering like that, I have not escaped entirely. I normally go through one or two weeks a year when I join the rest of humanity in the endless sniffling and eye watering madness.

This is probably why it took until high school for anyone to realize that, for some unknown reason, I am exceedingly hyper-reactive to the drug Benadryl. What a one-time mixture of shrooms, LSD and marijuana would do for other people, Benadryl does for me in one little dose.

This discovery was made on one fateful morning my junior year of high school when I woke up at my normal get-up time of 5:30 A.M. to prepare myself for the day and found that my head felt more stuffed up than a squirrel attempting to play Chubby Bunny with 100 marshmallows in its cheeks.

I blearily stumbled into the kitchen and found a bottle labeled; "Benadryl: Allergy Suppressant." Being in liquid form, I had to read the back of the box to figure out what my dosage should be.

There are very few things I am good at early in the morning. At 5:30 A.M. I am proficient at keeping most of the drool in my mouth and not tripping over the edge of the tub more than once as I clamber into the shower. I am not accomplished at reading anything more sophisticated than, "See dog run. Run dog run," that early in the morning, particularly when the font is tiny.

So I took the suggested amount, quickly got ready for school and hoofed it towards the bus stop. About halfway through the bus ride my brain began to review what I had read and the amount I had taken, and for some reason something didn't seem right. I shrugged my shoulders, and let it go. After all, I was feeling GREAT at this point.

I happily wandered towards my first class of the day, speech and debate, literally beaming at everyone I passed. This scared a lot of people. Thanks to one of my high school's head cheerleaders, who I had once informed that if she ever picked on mentally handicapped kids trying out for sports teams again I would replace her hairspray with mace, I had earned the nickname "Demon Bitch."

Her being more popular than I meant the nickname not only stuck, but to it was attached an entire persona that people, who had never met me before, were convinced I had. In real life I'm a fairly kind person with a sense of humor. Most people, thanks to the Cheerleading Brigade, thought I wore spiders in my hair and ate puppies for breakfast.

I can only imagine the absolute confusion, then, when the normally rather reserved and infamous "Demon Bitch," clad in black, randomly started walking up and hugging complete strangers in the middle of the hallway. It didn't matter who they were, I was feeling FANTASTIC and wanted to share the happy sensation to anyone and everyone I passed. My hugging spree ended as the bell rang for class to start and one of my friends found me hugging a trash-can goodbye.

My speech and debate coach was one of the most amazing people I have ever had the liberty of meeting. Herby Kojima, a beanie, yellow-tinted sunglass and goatee-sporting individual coached a team, which, for three years running, took nearly every competition we entered.

Very little made Kojima lose his cool, which is probably why, instead of calling the cops on me, he simply sat there with a confused smirk as he watched me debate an opponent in a mock round. As the round continued my statements got more and more confusing and less and less about the debate topic.

I have no memory of this round, but apparently I spent all of my cross-examination time asking my opponent where she had bought her shoes. My closing argument was eloquent, but basically boiled down to, "I should win because the purple mushrooms tell me so, coach."

After the round was over Kojima took me aside and calmly asked me what drugs I was on. I shook my head and slurringly informed him that I had taken Benadryl that morning. He blinked a couple of times, "Allison, I know you don't do drugs, so I'm going to trust you when you say that's what you took. How much did you take?"

I plastered a stupid grin across my face as I proudly informed him that I had gulped down four tablespoons of the liquid concoction that morning. His eyes widened a bit as he went to his computer to look up dosages. After few seconds of clicking around on the computer he turned back to me, "Allison, that is four times as much as someone your age should be taking!"

I was no longer listening; I was too busy being fascinated by the fact that I had toes. Kojima stood up and tried to get my attention, "Maybe you should just lie down."

At that point the shrill of our schools electronic bell system sounded, and I smiled saying, "Nope, gotta go to history now! Learnin' 'bout those presidents!"

Kojima sent one of my teammates after me as I proceeded to ricochet off the walls of the hallway like a pinball as I made my way towards history.

I made it to history and my teammate attempted to explain to my teacher Mrs. Chumbley that I wasn't doing too well. She looked over at me, weaving in my chair and hiccupping, and said, "Oh, I'm sure she'll be fine, we're talking about really easy stuff today anyways.

Mrs. Chumbley was her own kind of neurotically special. She was a wiry blonde woman with thin-rimmed glasses and a persistent need to emphasize everything she said with ecstatic arm motions and body twitches.

At one point during the semester we had been studying the South during the Civil War. Mrs. Chumbley, teaching right along, "And that is how the Union... Oh... Oh no... THE GRAVY!"

Mrs. Chumbley leapt across the room to our bemusement and began frantically dialing into her desk phone. We could all hear the receiver click as the other person came on the phone and Mrs. Chumbley nearly screamed, "THE GRAVY!"

Mrs. Chumbley was a little hard of hearing, so she had her phone turned up to the max level, which is how we were all graced with the sound of her husband's, "What?"

"Gravy! Microwave! It's been in there for three days!"

Then she hung up the phone, walked calmly towards the front of the room and just continued from exactly where in the sentence she had left off, "sacked Georgia."

Sitting in my desk, high out of my mind on Benadryl, I smiled and nodded at everything Mrs. Chumbley cared to comment on. At one point she noticed how strangely happy and attentive I was being, so she decided to direct a question to me. I began my answer, "Well, George Washington-" and then I passed out thudding my head on the desk with enough force to leave a bruise for days afterwards.

I have no memory of what happened next. I have been told the rest of the story by my friends. Apparently Mrs. Chumbley did not understand that I had just passed out, instead she made the assumption that I had died.

In a blind panic Mrs. Chumbley bolted over to her phone and began screaming into the receiver, without pressing any buttons,

"911! 911! 911!" until my very cool headed friend Mollie got up, poked me with a pencil and said, "We're good, she's just asleep."

I'm told I eventually sat back up and was somewhat responsive, and according to the attendance roster I went to the rest of my classes that day. I have absolutely no recollection of any of it. What I remember is waking up to the sound of my alarm the next day, getting ready for school and going to my first class only to be told it was Thursday and not Wednesday.

I also learned I had lost an entire day of my life in a haze of allergy medication when the known school druggy came up to me and asked, "So, what were you on yesterday? It sounded fantastic!?"

I spent the rest of my high school career being referred to as, "That girl who went on that crazy trip that one day and almost died in Mrs. Chumbley's class, you know, Demon Bitch?"

What kernels of knowledge can be picked from the cob of my experience?

1. Always quadruple check dosages on medications you've never taken before. Some meds can have serious side-effects such as liver damage, kidney failure or apologizing to doorframes after you've stumbled into them.

2. You can't win a debate via votes from drug-induced hallucinations, no matter how enthusiastic they are. However, you can take a nap under a desk somewhere and no one will bug you.

3. Don't do drugs, kids, people will poke you with sticks to make sure you're still alive.

20. I CAN'T WIRELESSLY PASS TISSUE

There are some things I wish someone had warned me about before I chose psychology as my field of study in college. First, I wish someone would have warned me that within a year's time I would be classically conditioned by one of my professors to salivate anytime I heard the name "Pavlov."

A heads up that within two years' time I would be making psychology related jokes to everyone I knew, regardless of their major, religion, sexual orientation or AAA membership status would also have been warranted.

Probably the most important tidbit of information, which slipped by me, was that by signing up as a psychology major I was implanting myself with a homing beacon for every random, distressed, psychotic or person with a funny aunt to find me. It was like the second I was registered for my "Introduction to Psychology Class" I somehow managed to acquire a giant neon sign with magical unicorns floating around it that read, "PSYCH MAJOR, DUMP HERE!" that everyone but me could see.

Now before you slam this book shut and storm off thinking that I am some heartless witch, I would like to state that there is a caring reason I got into psychology; research. Ok, maybe not a heartwarming conclusion to years and years of schooling, but in my own defense, it was research to help people.

Honestly, I really don't have a problem with sitting with someone and hearing them out when it comes to their problems, paranoid rants or story about how their airship will solve world hunger. However, there are a couple pieces of information which would be nice to have; namely what medications are they on or supposed to be on, and what their names are.

In college I actually kept a tally of people each week who randomly walked up to me and began telling me about their break-up/dead animal/best friend causing the break-up/sad book they read that they haven't been able to get over/family drama/break-up involving a sad book and family drama.

They would snag me as I walked to class, outside stores waiting for friends to finish paying for purchases and once inside a public restroom, and whop me upside the head with emotional baggage, often coming in a matching set. By the end of my undergraduate career my record was 11 people, I did not actually know, making me their impromptu confidant in one week.

It got to the point that if I saw a teary eyed individual anywhere in my vicinity I would automatically reach into my bag for the baggy of tissues I had to avoid getting another shirt wet.

The strangest of all these emotional assaults occurred in my freshman year of college.

That year I had a laptop that was the functional equivalent to a crack-crazed squirrel trying to run a Vaudeville act. I had owned my little PC for approximately five months, and thus far the wonder of modern mechanics managed to crash on me four times. "Scrappy the Crappy Computer," as it was dubbed, had to be overhauled with new system hardware twice, but even then it still ran about as well as I imagine Stephen King writing children's books with titles like "Jimithy the Happy Bunny," would go.

One day, I was doing the extremely complicated task of trying to open up one of my saved papers when a strange smell suddenly permeated my nostrils. My roommate at the time, Shawna, and I watched as little wisps of smoke began to curl out of the back of my huge honking laptop.

A bit alarmed I unplugged the machine and attempted to turn it off while simultaneously waving it around in the air to cool it off in a sort of whirling dervish. The immediate danger over, I called the number I had memorized at that point; tech support.

Going through the regular rigmarole I finally got transferred to someone in India. I happen to know he was from India because I asked him if he was anywhere near the area my Grandfather was traveling through at that point and he told me exactly which little town in India he came from.

In any case he began to put me through the, "Holy schnikeys your computer just about caught fire," troubleshooting process.

As we continued through the process we hit a point where there was going to be a 20-minute download of some kind or another. Knowing that if I let this guy off the phone I would never get another live person until the moon had turned to white chocolate truffles, I instructed him to stay on the line and started saying things like, "So, how are you?"

I would like to state that I never once mentioned that I was a student, or that I was studying psychology. I did not mention psychology in any way shape or format. There were no utterances of Freud, no ponderings by Pavlov, no theories by Erikson.

There was a little gasp on the other end of the line, and suddenly the tech support representative let out a little sob, "I'm berry berry sad!"

I then sat in wonderment as the man on the line took me through his very own Bollywood drama about how his estranged brother was trying to steal his girlfriend while he worked long hours here at tech support and his mother disapproved of his girlfriend and how he ate something bad for lunch...

My roommate peered curiously at me from across the room as I tried to interject at any moment I could, "Oh, well that's too ba- Uh-huh, your mother huh? Bad curry?" as the sounds of loud sobbing carried across the room over my phone. I eventually had to write a large sign explaining that I had a sobbing tech support person on the other line. She simply shrugged her shoulders and returned to reading her nursing textbooks. Lucky her.

Sure her major required her to work with blood, guts and oozy things. But I had to deal with verbally gushing individuals who were afflicted with emotional word vomit, and there was no biohazard suit in the world, which could save me from it.

Forty-five minutes later I finally got in a, "Well, I'm sorry that all of that is going on. I'm sure it will get better."

The man on the other sighed and said, "Is dat download complete yet?"

Truth be told it had been done for a good long while, but I didn't have the heart to tell him that I had nearly drooled into my phone now at least twice. After getting off the phone my computer was no closer to being fixed than Joe Pesci has of being a pro football player, however, I did have a new respect for the apparent powers that my major possessed.

What radioactive units of knowledge can be gleaned from this toxic spill?

1. Your major in college defines you. Whether you like it or not if you are an accounting major you will be asked to help with peoples' taxes, if you are a nursing major people will ask you about their weird rashes and if you are a philosophy major people will ask you what you're doing with your life.

2. If you have the problem of complete random strangers coming up and crying on your shoulder, wear spike-covered clothing. This is a deterrent that stops most, not all but most, would-be bizarre confidants.

21. ROCK ON PALCON

PALCON, an acronym that strikes fear into the hearts of conferences and events staff everywhere. Standing for the Pastors and Leadership Conference (or the Panicking Anarchy of Leaches Conference, which is much more apt) my fellow staff members and I watched, helpless, as over 250 pastors and their spouses descended on us for a week of prayerful insanity.

The conference was a wild conglomeration of special media presentations, large worship concerts and random people we had never met hugging us in a fit of religious fervor. A majority of the pastors and additional persons were sweet as Funfetti cake with Rainbow Chip frosting. Others, however, were more like sardines wrapped in kale.

Take for instance the pastor who brought in a PowerPoint, that I believe had been created back when computers were the size of whole buildings. Now, I am somewhat tech savvy, but even a person who programs computers for a living would have had issues synching this ancient PowerPoint onto a brand spanking new system.

The second I pulled up the file the entire system went more nuts than a group of squirrels on crack. The fonts were wrong, half of the words wouldn't show up and let's not even talk about the cheesy clipart pictures. Being the only one watching that building that day, there wasn't much I could do.

The client, who was probably alive when Mozart was still writing his number one hits, turned on me like a mongoose surveying prey. Then with a mighty wheeze his eyes widened as he yelled, "You ruined it!!!!!!"

Despite the fact that he was using technology that was practically antique, he looked to me to work the miracle that would force two incompatible things to work together. This was like trying to get a lion and a lamb to co-write and produce a psychedelic musical together; it wasn't going to work and whatever resulted from my attempts looked like a garbled mess of Russian (or possibly Swedish) song lyrics.

Having been unable to help that customer I left the room to "call some tech people," even though I knew they were about to tell me what I already knew. I wasn't out in the hall for five seconds when a pastor's wife stomped over to me glaring at my name badge. I quickly hung up my phone in preparation for the incoming request, or abuse, whichever.

I was prepared to hear something about a clogged toilet or a light burned out in one of the conference rooms. I was not prepared for the violent question of, "Why don't you have a basket!?"

What I wanted to say at that point was, "Because I'm not the Easter Bunny?" or "Because I quit my underwater basket weaving class before I learned how to tie them off?" Instead I blinked a couple of times and said, "I'm sorry, did you request a basket?" hoping to discover what kind of a basket this crazed preacher's wife needed.

Her face turned a lovely shade of violet as she yelled, "No! I did not request a basket, but there is supposed to be one here!"

I'm not exactly sure where in my job description I missed the part about needing to be psychic, but this is probably why it pays to read paperwork before you sign it.

After making my aghast apologies I ran into the nearest break room, grabbed a basket holding the coffee creamers and ran back out, praying she didn't need a snake-charmer's basket or one woven from the hair of a unicorn.

The woman looked over my humble whicker offering, and slanted disapproving eyes at me before snatching it out of my hands and stomping off.

This, ladies, gentlemen, and especially literate small animals, was PALCON.

The week continued much like this, the majority of our customers being a little too affectionate while the others spent their time nitpicking with all their might. However, nothing could have been better than the last night of PALCON.

The final gathering was a full concert with several speakers and various videos being shown throughout. Up on stage, for the special event, we had set up two multi-channeled robotic lights. Basically they were lights that could do a whole bunch of pretty colors, shapes, directions and sizes all controlled wirelessly in the back with a control panel. These lights were trained on a backdrop of a bush to make the bush look like it was on fire, it looked very Biblical.

Now, there is one major problem with the wireless receivers on these robotic lights, and that is that they can use their signal to penetrate anything, except water and Superman's chest.

Luckily Superman was missing. Unfortunately, if you have ever taken any form of human biology in school, then you would know that humans are chalk full of water. So when the 450 people were sitting, all was well and happy and the bush burned like it should. When they all stood up for the final prayer we had about 100 little bodies of water blocking off the signal to the robotic lights' receiver.

As the pastors rose solemnly for their final prayer, they all bowed their heads, as we up in the sound/lighting booth sighed in relief that this conference was almost done. But then we noticed as one of the robotics suddenly went from its intended bright orange, to a bright purple. Then, the one next to it turned from fiery red to a neon green.

Apparently, when robotic lights are no longer getting direction from the lighting board, they don't just sit quietly and hold the position that they have been holding for the past seven hours. No, instead, they act like a group of small children released in a candy store while on crack.

In horror/fascination/hilarity we watched as the head pastor soberly continued praying, "And dear Lord, may there be a blessing..." and the lights behind him launched into a multi-directional lightshow of their very own that would have been perfect for a disco rave party.

Flashing every color of the rainbow on every surface of our auditorium the lights went absolutely berserksies in a way no manner of button smashing at the light board could control.

We could definitely see who was praying with their eyes open, because heads all across the auditorium swept up towards the stage where the lights were now strobe lighting a mixture of bright pink and yellow across the otherwise rather dark room.

One of our technical crew was already headed up there and eventually he was able to reach the stage, the problem being that the pastor was still praying directly in front of our anarchistic lights.

This employee was, for approximately all his life, a Boy Scout, and being such, he did what any Boy Scout would do; he army crawled across the stage behind the praying minister in an attempt to unplug the rogue equipment.

Back in the booth the rest of the crew and I stood, slack jawed and saying little prayers of our own, as we watched our brave coworker attempt to pull the huge plugs out of the floor sockets while lying flat on his stomach as the lights moved on to do a swirling pattern on the ceiling as they flashed various colors. Our intrepid coworker yanked out cords with all of the speed and strength of The Incredible Hulk on meth.

The minister ended his prayer and lifted his head to see the stalwart employee backwards army crawling back off the stage to the applause of the few pastors who had both seen the event and had a sense of humor.

Later, after our boss was done repeatedly slamming his head into his office wall, he congratulated us on our collective ability to keep our cool. None of us had the heart to explain the difference between "keeping one's cool" and "being too panicked to move." We all had a hearty, deep, piratey laugh about it, approximately three and a half months later.

What lessons can we learn from this?:

1. Some jobs may require one to be psychic or at least extremely intuitive.

2. Never let robotic lights play on their own. They are far too immature to be trusted out in public.

3. Sometimes there is nothing one can do but stare at your own demise and laugh hysterically at it.

22. I THINK I'LL SHUT-UP NOW

Have you ever had one of those instances so bizarre you suddenly believe that you fell asleep and are dreaming? I have had this happen more times than Mel Gibson has said something offensive.

During my time working with a youth oriented non-profit organization, I had the opportunity to work with an outreach team, which was more fantastic than the thought of a thousand housecleaning elves. While, for the most part, the work was great, there were certain tasks my comrades and I had to undertake that were less than thrilling.

One such happening was, "Valley Fest," a totally whack job conglomeration of small screaming children, local dance troupes with varying degrees of professionalism, overpriced, yet wonderfully smelling, food and bright colors that would give someone with a hangover a migraine for life.

Our job, on that bright and exceedingly warm day, was to plant ourselves at a booth at this Valley Fest wearing obnoxious Kelly green shirts decorated with some stick figures. Three of us, Kari, Alex and myself, took the first four-hour shift of trying not to look more bored than if we were watching a sloth chew leaves.

The first few hours were pretty slow in a "we might as well have been the booth offering samples of anthrax and the black lung" kind of a way. As we sat there, feeling ourselves age, we surveyed the world around us as it stood. Directly behind our booth stood the food court, wafting incredible smells in our direction. We intensely resisted the urge to leave our post and invade the local Baklava stand carrying our organization's banner as a war flag. It was tempting, though.

In front of us was a medium-sized stage being used for local artists, dancers, failed comedians and the like who were supposed to be the entertainment for this whirling dervish of drivel.

As we sat there, I, in my ignominiable fashion, attempted to lighten the mood. I did this namely by pointing out that our plight could be worse by saying, "Hey, at least there isn't any polka music!"

The words had no sooner left my mouth than we heard the warming-up chords of an accordion drift through the air. I shrugged my shoulders as we all cringed in rhythm with the booming tuba driven German beat.

When the polka band eventually left, and we no longer felt like ripping the heads off of small stuffed animals, we returned to our previous activity of staring off into space, wishing that we could watch cement dry because then at least something would be happening.

Stuck in the vast expanse of nothing once again I turned to my coworkers and said, "Well, at least there are no interpretive dancers."

Alex, saying nothing, pointed a long arm towards the stage.

Kari and I stared as flamboyant leotard-clad women took the stage and began a new age interpretive dance, which made us all want to go out and rent Richard Simmon's *Sweating to the Oldies*, as it would have been far easier to watch.

At this point both of my coworkers were shooting sly glances in my direction, very possibly wondering where my crystal ball was hidden. Hoping to direct their attention away from the fact that I had apparently doomed us all twice, I noticed a bright multi-colored canopy that had been set up, but not occupied.

The empty canopy was a rainbow vomit of colors with streamers and a wonderful swirly pattern. The kaleidoscope of colors making it look a little like we were all about to be eaten by the happiest giant jellyfish on earth. We mused about what would be under there, and, half-jokingly, I said, "Well, I hope it isn't clowns."

At this time, I need to state something. I am not afraid of clowns. However, they do creep me out. I do not trust someone who always smiles, wears that much make-up and who dons so much ridiculous clothing, which is probably why I would never talk to one of the Kardashians.

The words had barely left my mouth when Kari turned and said, "Hey Allison, look."

Walking towards us, with their painted on smiles and confusingly huge pockets, were clowns.

It so very rarely happens that what one says almost immediately becomes a reality I found myself more startled by their approach than a person who opens up a package expecting candy and instead finds a rabid badger.

I stared, barely blinking, as the clowns strode up to me, their leader asking, "Hey, can we set our stuff here for a minute?"

Dumbfounded, all I could do was blink.

The leader clown turned to me, "Oh hell, you're not afraid of clowns are you?"

Kari started laughing. This did not help the predicament, because the clown then got angry, like a P.C. devotee who has just been told Macs are better. "I just don't understand why people are afraid of clowns!"

Then the lecture ensued. Had I all of my wits about me, or at least some still in the same county, I would have mentioned that being yelled at and lectured by a clown was not really helping the, "Don't be afraid of clowns," point.

Eventually the clowns left and I had enough of my soul remaining to turn towards Kari, who just shook her head and said, "You are not allowed to say another damn word while we're here, ok?"

Eyes wide as my face twitched, I nodded solemnly and shut up.

So what can we garner by rubbing through the make-up covering some wonderful knowledge?

1. The ringing in your ears caused by lots of tiny children's screaming voices and loud nagging parents will go away. You just have to be patient, engage in a steady diet of ibuprofen and wait a few days.

2. Stop while you're behind, because even if you are at the bottom of the pit already, someone can always throw you a shovel and instruct you to keep digging, and the bottom of the pit will probably contain clowns.

23. DUMB BLONDE

Most little girls dream of getting a puppy or a pony. I was the lucky girl who got both. No, I did not have two separate creatures, I had Resident Genius. Resident Genius, shortened to R.G. so that we could get his name out before he crashed into a china cabinet, was supposed to be a golden retriever mix.

Our theory is that he was mixed with one of the Budweiser draft horses. At six months old this puppy stood a yard tall. His tail alone knocked lamps off of tables and gave bruises based on his happy wagging. Probably the most noticeable thing about R.G., aside from the fact that he was monstrous, was he was a complete idiot.

Everyone expects puppies to be kind of gawky and goofy for their first few months of life; puppies galomp around the house, try their new teeth on furniture, occasionally forget that they need to pee outside and chase squirrels down the street.

R.G. would tear through the house like a hurricane, his giant paws making it sound like the four riders of the Apocalypse were upon us. We actually had to dive out of the way on occasion because, like a juggernaut, once R.G. built up momentum he was unstoppable.

Most puppies chew on furniture, and R.G. was no exception. However, whatever R.G. did, he tended to do in excess. One morning I came down into our living room and had one of those, "Something seems different in here," moments. It took me a second to realize it, but when I did, all I could do was stare like a burglar might stare at a person who owns a guard platypus.

When I had gone through the initial stages of shock I had to pull my mom into the room so she could join me in absolute awe. My mom wandered into the room, paused for an instant, and asked, "Where is the yellow chair?" The answer to that question was littered about the carpet and appeared in R.G.'s mountain sized droppings for about a week after he had managed to down the entire chair in one night. I think that's tantamount to the pace of about 15 competitive eaters packing down 50 plus hotdogs.

R.G., despite the fact that he could take on Godzilla and probably win, was a nervous puppy. Loud noises scared him more than sex scandals scare politicians. One could be yelling across the house for someone to pick up his or her laundry and R.G. would freak out, lose all control and start peeing.

R.G. had a spacious bladder, much like the fuel tanks for aircraft carriers. So, you'd grab him by the collar and, as fast as one could go with a puppy that weighed about as much President Taft, one would have to run for the back door. You'd run through the living room, piddle, piddle, piddle, through the kitchen, piddle, piddle, piddle, out onto the back porch, piddle, piddle, piddle, and onto the grass, where the floodgates to the Mississippi River would close, nothing. There was not enough Scotch Guard in the world to save our carpets.

Probably the most important part of my puppy's day was his chance to chase things. It didn't really matter what that thing was; squirrels, cars, innocent neighbors who were out watering their lawns, immobile telephone poles, he just had a desire to chase, catch and then demand affection from whatever he saw. Considering how big he was, this made walking him more difficult than trying to beat off a gang of apes armed with chainsaws with a single piece of string cheese.

It was on one such day, as I was headed out to take him for a walk, I suddenly realized I had left something inside. Not wanting to have to fight the beast to get him back into the house, I looped the handle of his leash over the top of one of our dug in, cement based, fence posts.

I came back outside a few seconds later to not only find no dog, but no two yard section of fence, either. R.G. had seen a possum (common in Georgia) and had decided to chase it. Whereas most dogs would be thwarted by a chain leash around their necks, R.G. had all the determination of Ralph Nader.

With Goliath strength he had ripped the entire section of fence out of the ground and was happily racing around the neighborhood after the possum dragging his past confinement along with him.

He never did catch the possum. However, I do wish to, in print, apologize to the person who owned the silver Toyota that R.G. actually did catch. Do you still need your hubcap back?

What can we learn by hacking through the brush in the jungle of experience?

1. Don't mess with a creature's nature, or he may make nature all over your living room.

2. Pets cost money, if not in things like food and collars, then in furniture, fences and carpet cleaner.

71

24. NOT THE NICKNAME I WAS EXPECTING

I have garnered many a nickname in my rather short lifetime. Some of them have been adorable, like my baby nickname "Squeaker." Others have been less adorable, like the one bestowed upon me in high school by a group of extremely angry cheerleaders "Demon-Bitch."

None of my nicknames have ever been acquired in such an odd manor, however, as the one I gained my fourth week of college.

I moved in as a freshman on a wing that was populated by half the volleyball team. Now, before I get shot for generalizing about volleyball players, I would like to say that I have met several capable, smart volleyball players. Most of these girls, however, were not among them.

One airhead in particular lived right next door to me. She was a tall, leggy girl with one of those giggles that reminded one of bubblegum and the fact that they forgot to go to their fake-tanning session last week. We'll call her Barbie for obvious reasons and she was, shall we say, special?

She was not special in the, "my mommy thinks I'm super talented and cool," kind of way. No she was more special in the, "I just decided to pimp out a 1990's Caravan complete with rims, hydraulics and spoiler," sense. Barbie was the kind of person who made you wince nearly every time she opened her vacuous mouth to spew something about Katy Perry's latest look.

The first time she met me and found out that I was a psychology major, she asked, "So, wait, you're going to learn to read peoples' minds?"

Blinking hard to make sure I wasn't having a, "I just started college eek!" stress dream, I simply stared at her.

Then two weeks into the start of classes, I was woken up in the middle of the night by a frantic knocking at my door. My roommate, a nursing major, was staying with her parents that weekend, so it was up to my lackadaisical butt to answer the heavily thudding door, which, of course, means I didn't.

However, the pounding persistently continued, much like the thudding produced by bad techno at every dance-club a drunk group of sorority girls has ever stumbled out of. I pulled my door open, barefoot and leopard print bathrobe clad, to find Barbie literally squirming in panic. She pushed past me into the room calling out, "So, is your roommate here!?"

"Umm... what? No, she's at her parentals."

"Well, I need to ask a nurse a question."

I did some more blinking. My roommate had been a "nursing major" for approximately two weeks now, which made her as well trained of a nurse as I was at being a professional penguin wrangler. I could only respond with a drowsy, "Well, I'm sorry she isn't here, bu—"

"Well, then I might as well ask you the question."

Yes, because I, as the four-week roommate of a two-week nursing major, would have any knowledge of diseases, germs and fungi. Even in my very groggy brain this made about as much sense as a giraffe in a bathtub full of lime Jell-O.

While my dumbfounded mind attempted to find a declaration that was both eloquent and kind, and not including the words, "3 A.M.," "crowbar," and "human skull," she piped up with her concern.

In rapid-fire verbiage she squealed, "So, I just peed green!"

"Wait, what?"

"I drank a bunch of blue Gatorade, and now I'm peeing green! Is that bad?"

Tired, dragged out of bed at a strange unholy hour and trying to figure out why her hair could possibly look that good at a time when even nocturnal creatures are yawning, the only thing I could physically bring myself to say was, "Oh no! That's the first sign! The aliens, they got to you too!"

Barbie's antics continued, with everything from me editing papers for her on which spell check had obviously never been clicked, to her repeatedly walking into my room and asking why I was sitting at her desk.

I tried to keep my sarcastic comments to a minimum, but once I discovered they went completely over her head, I just let them fly free like falcons preying on very fat, very slow, three-legged rodents.

By the way, you know that a paper you are editing for someone is going to make you want to cry when the first sentence reads, "The Egyptian pyramids."

The Egyptian pyramids do what? Do they look pretty compared a one-eyed sailor, do they tap-dance into our hearts, do they give free kazoo lessons!? Until I am told what The Egyptian pyramids do, the phrase is no more a sentence than a crippled turtle can compete in baseball.

I didn't bother to read the rest of the paper, I simply returned it to her with a purple frowny-face drawn at the top. At least I was kind enough to respond in her native language.

One day, actually during daylight, shockingly enough, there was a knock at my door and Barbie came in carrying a pair of skinny jeans that looked like they were made as a double sleeping bag for some garden snakes. Distraught, Barbie looked at me, holding the pants in front of her like they were humanity's last hope for world peace and rainbows, "I got jam on the crotch! Does jam, like, stain!?"

Sighing, I wordlessly took the pants from her, grabbed a trusty can of stain lifter and headed for the dorm laundry room. There I showed her how to use some warm water and a stain remover to, you know, lift stains.

She watched the entire process like I was some kind of sorceress, who had managed to learn the black magic of laundry and who was kind, but still a little terrifying.

Overjoyed that her pants had been returned to her wet, yet unscathed, she ran across the hall to her room, flung the door open and yelled at the top of her lungs, "She's just like a mom!"

I'm not really sure what Barbie's mom was like, but I severely doubt she was a short, weightlifting, loud, snarky Goth girl. However, despite the fact that I looked less maternal than a tyrannosaurus eating a triceratops carcass, I somehow found myself being called, "Mama Hawn," for the rest of the year by a majority of our campus' volleyball team.

This meant that I would be sitting in the cafeteria and a girl, who I could not have recognized with the powers of omniscience would, walk up to me and say something like, "Mama Hawn, do you know how to −insert mundane house task that apparently is no longer taught to children like vacuuming or spider killing-?"

I spent the rest of the year ducking anytime I saw the volleyball team march by, not out of fear of being recognized and waved to, but in fear of being recognized and ask to tie someone's shoe.

There are some important lessons that must be learned from my misadventure:

1. There is such a thing as a dumb question.

2. Answering one dumb question often can open up the door to an abyss, which releases all dumb questions upon you like a tidal wave. If you give a mouse a cookie, it will then ask you to get jam out of its pants, followed by the mouse taking a nap on your bed believing it is his or her own.

3. Yes, you can get strawberry jam out of pants.

25. CUSTOMER SERVICE

I often have friends and curious passersby ask me how I meet such a wide berth of absolutely bat-shit insane conglomeration of people. The answer is two-fold; I have a habit of talking to just about anyone who approaches me and I have lived, worked, traveled and been lost in some of the more interesting corners of the world.

With these two elements combined, it is really no surprise that I would have a few strange acquaintances staggering their ways through my life similar to a bundle of wounded apes. Still, I do tend to meet a lot more of them than the average, normal 9 to 5 person who enjoys romance novels and decorates their cubicle with puppy pictures that a working woman tends to. This is possibly because none of those things describes me.

Aside from the quantity, it really should be no surprise that I run into these people. One such person would be Travis, the bouncer who was mentioned in my recounting of trying to get a small Pentecostal through a rock concert alive.

I first met the bear/man when I was working for the classiest pizza place in the world, also known as Little Caesar's Pizza. Travis would be what happened if Paul Bunyan and a female body builder ever had a child. He was tall, tall enough that I once actually face-planted into his stomach.

Travis was my manager, which meant he usually left me to my own devices as he examined the inside of his eyelids in the back room. He was the kind of person whose work ethic could only be paralleled by that of a one legged sloth in a vat of cold maple syrup.

In fact at one point I looked out the front store windows to see Travis, who had gone outside for approximately his nineteenth fifteen-minute break that day, being escorted into a police car by two very angry looking officers.

Unfortunately for me, Travis and the keys to the store went to jail for a couple of days. So, Little Caesar's was open that night until 3 A.M. until I could finally locate another manager four towns over to come lock the place up.

Only later did I find out that Travis was caught smoking pot, in front of a liquor store on the busiest thoroughfare in town, with a police station no more than a mile away. Travis was basically an elephant with the brain of a comatose hummingbird.

There was one very handy quality to Travis, however.

One day I was working the front counter on my own and a thin, rather scruffy looking guy ordered a pizza, picked it up, and left. Ten minutes later he came storming back in yelling that his pizza had been served to him cold. This was a lie. He had personally watched me pull the pizza out of the oven, cut it, and put it in the box for him. Not to mention that when I opened the box to examine the "bad pizza" I found only the crust of one lonely, solitary piece.

I flatly refused to give the irate and rather dumb con-artist his money back. That is when he got nasty. Apparently, he believed that if trickery didn't work, then by golly he was going to beat that $6.05 out of my body with his tiny whispish arms. I adopted my best *Ferris Bueller's Day Off* teacher face and stared through the insults and death threats.

His yelling rants continued for about three minutes. He was getting so red in the face and furious that he didn't notice the thudding footsteps coming from the back room.

Travis came around the corner, reminiscent of a dragon recently awoken from a dream about eating horses drenched in ketchup.

Yawning, Travis leaned over my head, placed one, huge, hairy, tattooed arm on either side of my 5' 3" frame and glared at the customer who had suddenly stopped yelling. Travis sighed and said in a deep booming voice, "Can I help you, sir?"

I blinked, and in between the time my eyes closed and reopened from automatic lubrication, the man was gone, leaving behind the mostly empty pizza box and a swinging glass door that I was shocked hadn't come off its hinges.

What knowledge can be scraped from the oven-rack of experience?

1. Make sure that wherever you work has multiple keys for lock-up.

2. No matter how annoying a coworker is, they do have a useful purpose, even if it is scaring away someone even more annoying than he or she.

26. FIRE FROM HEAVEN

I am not a morning person, I'm more of a morning velociraptor. Without the judicial application of my morning coffee or a jolting shower, I am not really a reasoning, intelligent entity. Instead I revert to my most basic instincts such as foraging for food in cupboards that do not and will never hold food or bursting into the bathroom without checking to make sure no one is in there first.

My roommates throughout college learned the super important lesson of, "Never ever ever let Allison do anything more difficult than lumber towards the bathroom, go pee and wash her hands on her own in the morning prior to a shower or caffeine."

Once this lesson was learned they stopped having to catch me as I left and remind me that my underwear goes on the inside of my pants or that I should probably take my books to class and not a sword.

I have tried every method for waking up crisp and fresh, like a slice of dewy cucumber. I have gone to bed early, tried to get clean air in my room by cleaning out the air filters and discovered ways of silencing noisy neighbors living above me with the use of Vanilla Ice's *Ice Ice Baby*. No matter what I do, however, I wake up about as fresh as a 30 year old pork rind.

This is why, if you ever visit me in my natural habitat, you will see little sticky notes that will make sense to my horribly groggy mind about anything that is not in my normal routine that needs to be remembered.

You may laugh and say, "Come on, Allison, it can't be that bad."

And comments such as those are why I provide this cautionary tale.

During my junior year of college, I was living in an itty-bitty apartment on the first floor of a small complex that had a courtyard jointing all of the dwellings together. My friend Amanda was turning 20, and in celebration that she had survived longer than the average cat, I decided I was going to make her favorite kind of cake for her; chocolate chip pancakes.

Pancakes are not really an anytime during the day or night food though, so in my brain I came up with the brilliant idea that I should cook them in the morning and bring them over then.

My brain was so overjoyed with my clever plan that I did not take into account the fact that Amanda is one of those "gets up and attacks the morning like a ferocious beast, working out, eating a healthy breakfast and probably beating a MENSA member at chess, before stalking her way towards her first class like a tiger stalks a lame sheep" types of people.

Of course to properly beat a morning into submission, one must get up at an hour when no living thing should be awake. So it was that my alarm shrieked like a banshee lit on fire at around 5 A.M. for me to get up and make pancakes.

Please keep in mind that I am the type of person who, throughout my sleeping hours, if I get too warm, might lose her shirt in her sleep. Also mull over the fact that at such an early hour I really do not think about things like, "Maybe I should open a window for some ventilation because the oven creates a lot of heat."

Nope, instead I stumbled my way into the kitchen, grabbed my only skillet, a cheap aluminum contraption, and began to stir together ingredients that I was pretty sure were for pancakes.

I'm not sure what caused the calamity I soon faced. Maybe cheap cookware plus butter and PAM is a deadly mixture. Perhaps instead of chocolate chips I managed to add little pieces of dynamite. In any case, I turned away to do something super important, like try to remember the word for the things that cover our windows, and when I returned my attention to the stove I was greeted by the lovely glow of fire.

A sane rational person at this point would have thrown the burning dish in the sink and turned on the water, or put a lid on the pan and choked the fire of oxygen. I, however, am not a sane rational person in the morning.

My first thought, after, "Ooooh! Pretty!" was that I needed to do something with the fire. I then realized we had a smoke alarm, which I might set off. That's right, my brain did not go "fire out, clear smoke later," my brain leapt like a gazelle on a trampoline to, "smoke alarm goes off, I get fined."

I can only imagine the sight my neighbors around the apartment courtyard caught if they overheard my violent cries of, "Oh shit! Oh shit!" I envision looks of amusement yet fear as they watched me, in Pink Floyd pajama pants and a sports bra, holding a flaming pan over my head, as I ran around in little circles.

It was only after my third or fourth lap of the courtyard that my brain finally kicked in with the, "Put the fire out, you dipshit!" command.

Chucking the pan into the courtyard's birdbath may not have been the most graceful moment of my life, but it did the trick, and I did not get fined.

What can be learned from my experience?

1.Even the simplest task can turn into a fireball.

2. If you are not a morning person, for the love of Pete, don't try to do anything until at least the sun has come up over the hills and slapped you in the face a few times.

3. Charcoal pancakes are really hard to get out of cheap cookware.

27. DAVENO OF DEATH

I have a family which could possibly rival the Adams Family in bizarre aspects. After all one does not get to grow up to be like me without having a few nuts in their family tree. I probably am one myself.

One such member was my Great-Grandmother Jesse. Great-Grandma Jesse was approximately the same width as a doll made from pipe cleaners, but whatever she said was what happened. She could give the stank eye from across the room and you could feel every fiber of your being freeze over like a chipmunk caught in a blizzard.

Great-Grandmother Jesse had lived through the Great Depression, and much like those who existed in that era she was reticent to throw anything away. After she died we found a can of Hershey's powder that had literally exploded due to age and decomposition.

Great-Grandma was on her third marriage, having survived her previous two husbands. The husband she had at that time she had met and picked up at a garage sale, kid you not.

On one of my "family vacations," when I was around eleven, my mother decided to visit Great-Grandma because my maternal grandparents were staying there as well.

When we arrived we found that my grandparents had gone out to run some errands, but Great-Grandma had kindly prepared dinner for us; a noodle soup with some veggies and chicken in it. My mother, brothers and I munched on the soup all of us giving it curious looks.

Something did not taste right. Even my brothers, who were five or six years old at the time and regularly ingested things like dirt, looked at the soup like they weren't quite sure whether to eat it or somehow sneak it towards the trashcan. None of us dared to say anything about it though under the watchful eye of Great-Grandmother.

My mother got a call on her cell phone and left the table to answer it. She came back saying, "You know what, I forgot, we already ate dinner, none of us need to eat *anymore.*"

I later found out the call was from my grandparents. The soup we were eating had been sitting on the stove for about four days, which is why they decided they needed to go run some "errands."

A hasty message passed from my mother in Pig Latin, and all four of us miraculously were suddenly full. We spent the remainder of the "meal" attempting to spread our food out in as thin a layer as possible to make it look like we consumed more than we had. During this time Great-Grandma was telling us where in the house we would be sleeping.

"Let's see, CarolBeth you can have the guest room... the boys can sleep on the sofa... yes... and Allison... I think you should sleep on the Daveno in the back room... yes... that is where my second husband died you know..."

My mother and I exchanged glances of sheer, "uh-oh" as we desperately both tried to remember of what affliction her second husband had died.

We didn't get much time to deliberate, however, as she suddenly stood and informed us that it was bedtime. There was no arguing with Great-Grandma Jesse. It didn't matter if you were five or thirty-five, she could send you to bed faster than Jell-O can be flung by a monkey on crack.

The back room at Great-Grandma's house was the most terrifying room I have ever been in. Not only was it the room that someone had died in, but it is possible that the room itself was the cause of death. The entire room was Pepto Bismol pink with deep matching shag carpet and shelves lined with dolls everywhere.

Having seen "Chucky" when I was four, I already hated dolls, and here I was faced with an army of little ceramic hands and faces on all sides.

Attempting to avoid the dolls at all costs, I moved towards the center of the Daveno.

For those who are unaware of what a Daveno is, imagine a bed that folds up in the center. Much like a futon, the contraption usually has a lock that stops it in some approximate way so that it looks like an oddly angled sofa.

As I inched closer and closer to the center of the bed, I began to hear a soft creak. I reached the center and the creak became a "SNAP!" as the Daveno slammed closed, bypassing the sofa-shape locks and proceeding to catch my entire body in a bear-trap-esque manner.

Consumed by the smell of dust and countless yard sales, I found myself in a predicament that my eleven-year-old self was not prepared for by after school T.V. specials. The Daveno was a tad shorter than I was, so the only things protruding from this metal and hellfire filled contraption were my feet and my hands; Allison taco.

I have had many near death experiences spanning from falling off of a roof to accidentally insulting the hairiest woman I have ever seen. None of those experiences, however, can explain the sheer terror, which, at such a young age, I faced, possibly dying in a piece of furniture that had already had the honor of one person kicking the bucket in.

Eventually I was able to wriggle myself free, brought my mother into the room to show her that her first-born child had almost been killed by decades old furniture and insist she scoot over and let me have half of guest room bed. From that point on, that entire trip was referred to as, "The Daveno of Death."

So what can creaks of knowledge we learn from my crypt seeking adventures?

1. If the soup tastes funny, it is appropriate to ask in which decade it was made.

2. Pepto-Bismol pink is possibly the most nauseating color for interior design.

3. If someone has died on a piece of furniture, always inquire as to whether the piece of furniture was the cause of death before sleeping on it.

28. HOW I SURVIVED THE LITHUANIAN DEATH FLU

I don't often get sick. I have an iron constitution reinforced by the fact that I'm kind of addicted to oranges, garlic and exercise. When I do get sick, however, it's a doozey, much like the first step taken out of an airplane hovering over Guatemala during a hurricane. I have a mostly missing small intestine to prove it.

My senior year of college I made it the entire year without even so much as a case of the sniffles until about two months away from graduation. It began with feeling a tad fatigued and ended with the sensation of having been trampled by a herd of drunken Schnauzers driving dump trucks.

I avoid doctors (A) because they cost a ton when you have the cheapest insurance on the planet and (B) because I hate being told things I already know.

Very rarely have I been to a doctor's office and had them say something that was not more obvious than the fact that Charlie Sheen is about as insane as a troupe of drunken mimes. I once broke my arm in three places and the first thing the doctor did, after moving it around painfully like the arm on one of those bendy rubber toys and taking lots of pretty x-ray pictures, was to say, "Well, that seems to be broken. That's going to be painful."

And this is why you went to school for that big diploma huh, bub?

The week progressed with my general demeanor showing more and more signs that it might not be safe to release me amongst the general population. The first major sign of this was that I fried my phone. Now, you may be saying to yourself, "Come on, people fry their phones all the time in perfectly mundane ways!"

Well first of all, congrats for using a GRE word like "mundane" in an everyday thought. The way I fried my phone was not the normal "accidentally dropping it in a toilet" or "putting it in the microwave instead of your food," way.

I am a light sleeper, and, due to a certain demon bird outside my window, I had started wearing earplugs while I slept. This meant that when my alarm, a.k.a. my phone, went off, I could no more hear it than Tom Cruise could grow an inch taller. My solution was to put the phone on vibrate and stick it in my sports bra.

That night my fever, which I had been carefully trying to keep low, broke 100 degrees. When I awoke I found that my phone's battery had been unable to deal with the Sahara Desert heat wave. So, in essence, my boobs fried my phone.

Try explaining that one to the Verizon representative. I did, and several awkward moments later when he stopped blushing, I got a replacement phone.

Another indication of my illness was when my very good friend Annie, who is now a nurse, looked at me and said, "If you don't get your butt to bed right now, then Shayna, Amanda and I will drag you up there and duct tape you to it."

Since she is normally a nonviolent person, I took this to mean she actually believed I was ill.

At one point I slogged my way upstairs to get a book that I needed to read for a class, but when I got up the stairs I totally spaced on what I was looking for.

This was worse than losing my keys, or forgetting the name of a casual acquaintance. This was a total mind blank that left me more confused than a group of *Jersey Shore* cast members in a library.

Due to fever, and some random medications I had taken to dull my full body throbbing pain, I wasn't thinking the most logically at that point. I knew that I had come upstairs for something, something small, something I needed.

Squinting about the room as if narrowing my eyes activated some super memory bestowing vision, I stood in the doorway for a few minutes before alighting on the answer. I began searching through the room to find the obvious object of my quest.

After a bit my roommate downstairs got worried because I had been gone a while now for such a simple task, and things were far too quiet upstairs. She found me in our shared room digging through a drawer frantically.

"Allison, what are you looking for?"

"That damn leprechaun!"

"Umm... you came up for a book, wait, what leprechaun?"

My drowsy and ill brain had decided that the item I must be searching for was a small purveyor of either beer or marshmallow cereal, because who doesn't need a leprechaun, right?

I held out going to the doctor for quite some time, but just like Custer's last stand, I was doomed for failure. Granted, my failure didn't end with me being filled with arrows.

Then came the day when my roommate, and a vast majority of my friends, went to compete at a track meet two towns over. I decided that I had been too lazy that week and should get up to do some housework.

I think I got a whole fork washed before I suddenly felt like someone had just hit me in the stomach with a fleet of Fed-Ex vans driven by evil pixies. Deciding that I had been productive enough for one day, I assumed the position of sick people everywhere; namely curled up in a ball examining how fascinating my toes are while on a sofa.

My natural body temperature is one or two degrees below the average person, which, for those who skipped health class a lot in high school, means that a fever for me is normal temperature for your average sicky. So when I took my temperature I was slightly alarmed by the fact that the thermometer was announcing something a bit over 104.

I say only "slightly alarmed" because at that point I felt like the toilet in a trucker stop, so it wasn't an utter surprise. I tried to get up, but just like in the nightmares I have about being stuck on Freud's couch being repeatedly asked the question, "Why do you like cheese?" I found that I actually couldn't budge.

Luckily, as a member of my generation, my new non-boob-cooked cell phone was nearby and I was able to call someone to come get me and take me to a doctor.

Prying myself out of that chair to go to the car took more effort than trying to get all of the gum out of a New York taxicab floor, but I finally made it.

No matter what happens to me, or how wildly inappropriate it is, the one thing that always sticks with me is my sarcastic, and often morbid, sense of humor. It's the way I deal with things like strange dates or being chased by turkeys.

The intake nurse, a rather old no-nonsense type woman, at the "doc in the box" I arrived at, took one look at me and said, "You're sick."

I shook my head, "Nope, I thought I'd just stop by for the free tongue depressors."

The nurse who was tending to me apparently had never had a patient who could both be miserable and cracking jokes at the same time. She would ask me questions and then when I'd give some snarky reply would look at me like I was barbequing a kitten.

She led me down a hall to a waiting room. By "led" I mean she walked in front of me as I clawed the wall trying not to fall down. I entered the examination room and she turned to me with a tiny specimen cup about the size they serve juice to kindergarteners in and said, "We'll need a urine sample."

Now for those who may be reading this who are not female let me explain urine samples and women to you. "Urine sample" roughly translated into women speak means, "try really hard not to pee on your hand."

I stood, and by stood I mean leaned against the doorway grasping it with all my strength, and looked down at the tiny cup. The nurse looked at me expectantly like I needed to take it. I watched as the room began to rock back and forth. The nurse became a bit impatient, "Well, go on then."

I blinked a couple of times and finally said, "This may be the Wild West, but in my condition I am no sharp shooter."

She got me a bigger cup.

After waiting in that fluorescently lit room with the table covered in butcher paper for approximately three and a half centuries the doctor made his appearance. He walked in and the first words out of his mouth were, "You're sick."

At this point I was too out of it to do more than cough in his general direction. I finally got the energy to ask, "So have you found out what I have?"

The doctor paused a second then said, "Well, no, but we've canceled out three things that it could be!"

Fabulous out of how many thousands of diseases I could have, this man, with medical degrees, managed to knock out a grand total of three of them. I hate to point it out, but I could do that too; I know I didn't have lupus, the plague or tuberculosis.

After another eternity of waiting on the table the doctor came back again. "Well, we're not really sure what you have, take these pills and call us if you don't feel any better. We'll call you if we find anything."

My faith about as firm in doctors as it is in a giant floating green bean in the sky, I allowed myself to be driven home and plopped onto a couch. I proceeded to spend the rest of the weekend staring at random spots on the wall and wondering if they wanted to be my friend or not.

Finally on day five of the fever, after being told by every professor that I had, and a couple that I didn't actually have classes with, that if I came into class this sick they would kill me with a textbook, my fever dropped below 100. It took me a month to fully recover from all the symptoms of my mystery disease.

The doctors never did figure out what I had, which leads me to the conclusion that my fever, upset stomach, cough, inability to think a solid thought and constant bad bed hair were some new form of disease.

I have dubbed my illness the Lithuanian Death Flu, because Lithuania doesn't receive enough attention in the world. Please if you suffer from similar symptoms, throwing up innocuous water and hallucinating small mythical creatures, don't do what I did: don't stick your phone in your sports bra.

What lessons can be learned from my encounter with the Lithuanian Death Flu?

1. A sense of humor is not always appreciated. This is especially important to keep in mind if the victim of your jokes is someone who will be poking you with random needles.

2. Baffling medical science is much like baseball; three strikes and they send you out to take a hit and miss smattering of pills and hopefully get better.

3. If you have forgotten what you are looking for, the answer is seldom leprechauns.

29. SMEXY

In college a majority of my friends were on the track team. This is probably due to the fact that my university was pretty tiny and half of the school was the track team.

I was friends with pole-vaulters, long distance runners and had a roommate who could throw a big piece of metal on a string far enough to effectively drop invading knights on horses before they could charge.

I'm not non-athletic, but most of my sports have not made it on the track roster. Had there been a track and field event involving football, weight lifting, boxing, martial arts or being able to twiddle one's toes then I would have joined too.

I found most track events and their participants as befuddling as the idea of naming a child "Bookcase." My friends Amanda and Ashley would run with long poles in hand and somehow magically fly over a bar high above everyone's head with style as I gaped, searching for the anti-gravity devices they must be using, when walking out the front door I can barely clear the curb on a regular basis.

I would ogle on at track meets as javelin throwers, like Charlie, would neatly arc their ancient weapons and spear the ground, and, once, an unfortunate duck. Alicia and Shayna would throw metal discs as I prayed on the sidelines that their aim was good, lest someone die.

The ones that mystified me the most, though, were my friends who were sprinters or runners. These were people who volunteered to do something most of us have to be bribed to do on a regular basis.

I am diametrically cut in half, my legs are as long as my torso, which means that when I run one can almost hear the "Miniminiminimini!" noise that short cartoon characters make when they pad after their taller counterparts.

I would stare, slack-jawed as Annie would run more gracefully than a panther and leap over the hurdles in an arc that made dolphins look downright clumsy in comparison. I would gaze upon Caleb who could just continue running around the track like the Energizer Bunny on speed, and my only thought was always, "How!?"

The thing that amazed me about the runners, aside from actually liking to run, was their appetite, particularly the male distance runners. I would sit at a table full of track people and watch on in awe as plates upon plates of food would disappear into the black holes of their stomachs.

I once watched one of our long jumpers, Stephen, who was built like a lightning rod, down four sandwiches in one go. Standing up from the table, I stared as he packed two more sandwiches into his bag because, "I'm just gonna get hungry in an hour anyways."

One of these, Caleb, who is probably my friend mainly for the reason that we both enjoy messing with people, was the most impressive of them all in the appetite aspect. Standing at around six feet Caleb is about as big around as SlimFast Shake.

Every meal that he ate in my presence was like watching some horrible accident involving a train, helicopter and car full of clowns; you couldn't look away and weren't sure whether to laugh or not.

On one such day, Annie and I congenially ate while we watched as Caleb downed roughly enough food to satiate the hunger of every animal in the San Diego Zoo. As we chatted and counted how many burgers Caleb was downing, I happened to look at the table next to us and realized that there was an entire table of freshmen girls who were staring at Caleb all googly eyed.

I clandestinely pointed this out to both Caleb and Annie. Caleb, not really interested in the attention of giggly girls three or four years his junior, began the process of thunking his head on the table in between munching on fries.

We continued to converse at our table, but it seemed that every time we looked over at the other table the number of twitterpated girls grew. With each successive lass added to their group, the giggling grew louder and the staring became more obvious. Caleb began to shrink lower and lower in his seat, hunching over like he might want to start a new profession at the Notre Dame Cathedral as a bell ringer.

Caleb had finally finished the first six courses of his meal and was ready for dessert. That day dessert at the Dex, famous for food that made one wonder what their parent company was smoking, was an almost fluorescent blue cake. The entire thing looked like one might actually be eating the remains of hundreds of students' old highlighter pens.

Caleb picked up his fork and looked at the cake, amidst chattering and giggles from his own private audience. I looked at

Caleb, as he glanced back at Annie and myself with a, "What do I do?" expression plastered on his exceedingly expressive face.

Somehow our table conversation had turned to dinosaurs, most likely in relation to *Jurassic Park*. Half-jokingly I said, "You know, you could just take a page out of the velociraptor's book..."

The gleam that leapt into Caleb's eyes could only be matched in madness by a pyromaniac about to light a pile of fashion magazines on fire in the middle of a Hollister store.

He turned giving the ninny-headed group a smirk that was evil and dastardly to the core, put two fingers on each hand out like claws, turned and chomped down into his cake.

The blue carnage that ensued put the entire *Saw* series to shame, as Caleb began to devour the cake without the use of his normal eating appendages.

There was a small collective gasp from the next table over, and then there was silence, blessed silence.

Caleb, the philosophy and theology major, the long distance track runner, the high GPA holding velociraptor, finally pulled his face away from the plate of cake.

Blue frosting was stuck in his goatee, eyebrows and eyelashes as his cheeks poofed out with the pressure of nearly an entire piece of cake behind them. Smiling through the sugar and butter concoction Caleb turned back to the girls, waved one of his claw shaped hands and called out through the cake, "Hi dere!"

And they were gone. Their exit was faster than a greased bunny being slid across a linoleum floor, accompanied by Annie and my raucous laughter.

That day I picked up several important tips from Caleb:

1. Blue frosting is almost impossible to get out of one's facial hair.

2. Acting like a dinosaur in public can stop unwanted advances by the opposite sex.

3. If you run over 20 miles every week then stuffing an entire piece of cake in your mouth and downing it will have absolutely no effect on your waistline. Jerk.

30. INTROSPECTION TIME

Having once been an undergraduate college student, I look back on my years of learning and realize, much like a tissue-encased fly grasps its coming demise by the whirring noise of the toilet flushing, that there were not just individuals who bugged the living daylights out of me. No, instead there were certain types of individuals who annoyed both the living and the nonliving daylights out of me.

As I have opened a dialogue concerning these "types" of people, I have gotten an overwhelming response from others who have noticed the *exact* same things.

For those starting college, or maybe who have completed their degree and may find this commemorative, I have classified these groups of people who seem to appear everywhere we don't want them to.

Type 1: *Precious*

I had several of these, having gone to a private, rather conservative, university. These are the people that you look at, from a distance, out of the corner of your eye and immediately you know, "Home schooled."

Now before I get any angry letters defending home schooling I would like to state that I have met several well-adjusted individuals who were home schooled and who have gone on to lead productive and happy lives being doctors who make way more money than I do. Damn them.

No, the home schoolers that I refer to are the "Raised in a box, have never heard of the Beatles, believe that Harry Potter is Satanic and actually think that if you support Obama then you might as well support Joseph Stalin and Osama Bin Laden, no matter that they're dead and had completely differing ideologies."

I have labeled this group of individuals *Precious* because whenever they open their mouths in a class you will have the insane urge to say, "Awwwwwww..." pat them on the head, give them a cookie and send them towards their nap mat.

Take for instance my junior year of college when I took a Criminology class. In it we had a girl, whom my friends and I actually nicknamed "Precious" due to the fact that she both looked and acted like Shirley Temple.

We would be having a serious discussion on how crime could be prevented through community action and this girl would pipe up with, "Well, these people wouldn't be criminals if we didn't label them as criminals, we should try to label them something else, liiiiiiike lawbreakers." At which point everyone in the class would blink a few times and resist the urge to go buy her a lollipop.

Type 2: *Belligerent Militants*

These individuals are the exact opposite of the cute cuddly members of the *Precious* cult. These individuals not only have a chip on their shoulder, but a water buffalo with diarrhea, and they want the world to know it.

You will be sitting in class, listening to a wonderful lecture on something intelligent, or drooling asleep on your desk, your choice, and suddenly from the back of the room you'll hear, "Well that's not the way it is in my experience!"

Before you know it, this person has launched into a 40-minute lecture/rant/conspiracy theory of her or his very own. The professor will attempt to interject, but this will be a futile measure, for once the barrage has started it will not end until the simian-like attacker has run out of verbal poo to throw.

Like a horribly cheesy action flick where the hero never runs out of bullets, this person will fire away into a spiel that covers every topic from their own experiences of wrongdoing to how the subject in question is actually a ploy by the government to direct our attention away from the real issue of CIA sanctioned penguin torture.

The BM will go from their normal skin color, to red, to purple, then to a color you're not sure you've ever seen before, until they finally sit back in satisfaction that they have gotten their strange depraved point across.

In the same Criminology class as Precious, we had a BM who we called "Nails of Justice." This was mostly due to her exceedingly long talon-like nails that were painted a different shade every week. However, it was also in part to the fact that Nails of Justice was going through this class to help her gain certification as a court clerk in some county in the middle of nowhere in Oregon.

Nails of Justice had an opinion on everything in the class, and it all linked back to her tiny little county in Oregon. Someone would say something about the national crime rate being on the rise due to economic issues and she would pipe up with, "And if Burt's Ice Cream Shop hadn't gone outta business, I tell you the crime rate wouldn't have gotten so high!"

If anyone dared try to remind NOJ that we were talking about things on a national or even international level she would start clicking her looooooong nails against the table like a rattlesnake's warning rattle. If the person persisted she would eventually interject with something so wild and half-baked that you didn't dare refute it because you might set something amiss in an alternate reality somewhere.

"Why yes the federal government is important, but if it wasn't for the bat guano from our caves in Rinkadink, Oregon that helps fertilize the crops in the mid-Western states that also produce corn syrup that helps our soldiers become stronger and fight off Communism using weapons also made in Rinkadink, Oregon..."

By the end of her miniature rant we would all be exhausted, our mental powers completely diminished as we attempted to use the logical parts of our brain to chase her through and around the rabbit holes.

The only defense against this type is absolute silence, or possibly pepper spray laced with cyanide.

Type 3: *Personal Soap Operas*

Personal Soap Operas, (or PSO's to save me from carpel tunnel syndrome) are probably the most widely recognized types of people that make you want to scream and throw a live raccoon with rabies at them.

It does not matter what topic is brought up in class, work or in casual conversation, if there is an instant where the person speaking takes a breath the PSO will pipe up, spreading misery like the flue carried by speed enhanced gerbils.

These individuals also have no grasp or perspective on the comparative nature of tragedy, to them their gloom is the worst in the world.

Take for instance the classmate who I will call girl in the iron brace. If you ever spoke with this girl, you would find that she had maladies which would put people dying of liver failure to shame. She constantly wore two wrist braces and would insist people help her with even the most mundane task.

This person claimed that she could not write her notes herself, so the university had to set someone up to take notes for her. This person, a volunteer, then got to watch in wonder as this girl would pull out a journal during class, completely ignore the lecture, and write furiously the entire class period.

During the disasters that hit Haiti, a professor of mine, who knew several people in Haiti, asked all of us to keep the people suffering in the disaster stricken place in their thoughts, prayers and meditations. She then proceeded to ask if anyone else had anything that was going on that the students felt the rest of the class should be aware of.

What the professor meant was to ask if anyone else knew of other global disasters or crisis we should be aware of. What she got was the girl in the iron brace who nearly jumped out of her seat as her hand shot towards the ceiling with such force that several people surrounding her must have felt the shock waves as they all leapt back in surprise.

My professor, having had experience with this individual, looked around the room for any other hands. Seeing none, she let out the air in her lungs and raised a hesitant hand to let this person speak.

The PSO let out an overly dramatic sigh, "Well, *I* personally have been having some problems with my sore wrist, and that's making it hard for me to take notes, which is making it hard for me continue with my baton twirling..."

The tidal wave of suffering flowed forth for nearly 20 minutes as my professor, who was too polite to interrupt the PSO, began to twitch.

After that day that girl was never called on again. My professor would ask if there were any comments or questions and would gaze around the room as this girl almost danced the *Time Warp* to be noticed. If no other hands were up she would turn back to the PowerPoint with a little snap in her step, "Moving on to *actual* social issues."

Type 4: *Exacerbating Storyteller*

The Exacerbating Storyteller is closely related to the Personal Soap Opera. The difference is that instead of spreading tales of woe, they just spread constant stories.

You could be talking about ancient Chinese art that depicts bamboo forests and these people will be right there to tell the story about how they once, when they were twelve, they think, had some soup with some bamboo shoots in it.

It does not matter how thin the link is between their story and the topic under discussion, they will share some mundane snippet of their life with everyone every chance they get. These are the people that make you want to eat ibuprofen, like chocolate chips, straight from the packaging.

At one juncture I had a girl in a history class who told so many stories that other students and I would take bets to see how long the professor would allow her to talk before cutting her off mid-stream.

Her stories ranged from the downright boring to utterly pointless. She once somehow managed to get from our lecture topic of World War II to how her grandmother taught her to knit when she was five. The final record set was an hour of storytelling out of our hour and a half long class.

Type 5: *Living Onomatopias*

For those who did not have to read the dictionary as a small child, an onomatopia is a word that describes a sound such as, "Bang," "Pow," "Ftang" or any other comic book background bubble word that you can think of.

Living onomatopias are the people who, without saying a single word, create so much noise that it feels like the verbiage describing their act is slapping you upside the head.

These people can have a minor habit, like cracking their joints continuously, which at first does not bother you. As time continues, however, and whatever you are listening to becomes less and less interesting, it will begin to get under your skin worse than little sand crabs getting into your bathing suit.

Then again, the habit can be less minor, such as the person who insists on moving every bit of crud in their throat up into a more comfortable position. What this usually results in is a fifteen-minute battle that makes your classroom sound like a scene from one the *Alien* movies.

I actually had a guy fully hork something up in the middle of a class my sophomore year of college. His girlfriend broke up with him soon after. Was that the cause? Judging by what we all got a glimpse of as he bent over that wastebasket, yes, yes it was.

So what nuggets of knowledge can we mine from the caverns of my classification experience?

1. Check to make sure you are not one of these people, it will end poorly for you.

2. If you encounter one of these types of people your best option is to simply ignore them. If that fails, a can of hairspray and a lighter may be your only hope.

31. WHEN FUNFETTI CUPCAKES ATTACK

Out of all of the concerts, conventions and random clogging shows that I had to work while employed for the convention center, there was one type of performance that would make everyone on our production crew wince like we were having our toes stepped on by very fat ponies: ballets.

Ballets are a pain in the patoosky for several very labor intensive, drive you to start drinking anti-freeze in your time off, ways.

First there is the Marley floor, which is basically a giant black rubber floor that not only has to be stretched, stomped on, pulled and taped, but also cannot be ripped while any of those actions are happening unless you have thousands of dollars in your back pocket to order more Marley floor.

This process, with ten people, took more time than it takes one person to learn how to balance a plate of live crabs on a stick on top of their head.

Then there was the lighting, which had to be *perfect*. Of course, the definition of "perfect" changed from the director, to the performers to the performers' mothers.

After the hundredth time of hearing, "And my little Suzy needs to be spotlighted in pink for her three and half second solo dance move…" the other lighting designers and I formed a habit of nodding our heads while thinking about more important things, such as "How much wood *could* a woodchuck chuck if a woodchuck could chuck wood?"

Finally, there were the ballerinas themselves. One particular production featured 150 dancers; 45 of which were younger than five years old, and a grand total of six of which were male. With this much estrogen and glitter in one tiny theater I'm surprised we could all breath.

We made it through the rehearsal with the entire crew saying, "aww" as little ballerinas, dressed up as pumpkins, planted themselves for the fairy Godmother to dance around. We cooed at the little girls, donning the outfits of spring flowers, twirled, mostly in the same direction, to the music. And then we all stared in puzzlement at the next group of little girls who took the stage.

Ballerinas wearing the brightest rainbow 1980's carpet pattern I have ever seen trotted on stage. The crew collectively spent the entire rehearsal of the number debating what these little girls were supposed to be. It was finally decided, even though it made no sense in the context of *Cinderella*, these girls must be Funfetti cupcakes.

During the dress rehearsal the older ballerinas helped keep the little ones entertained and quiet as the stage crew went about fixing lights, checking sound and walking with purpose in a random direction so that parents couldn't grab us and insist that we somehow slow down the music so that their little darling could be on stage longer. You think I'm kidding. I pity you.

Later that evening we were all set for the show. I was on a communication headset backstage right, while another coworker of mine, Karissa, was backstage left with the same set-up. These headsets were important, not only to keep in contact with our fellow crewmembers up at the booth, but to keep us from being bored out of our tiny little skulls.

Unfortunately, these headsets had a cord, which meant that we were on a leash that was shorter than one of the seven dwarves.

My assigned position meant that I had several set pieces, such as a fireplace on wheels, that had to be moved out on stage at exactly the right moment.

Because the munchkin ballerinas were to be on stage for quite a bit of the first act, they were left backstage with, you guessed it, Karissa and I. We spent a lot of time saying things like, "Don't climb on the pumpkin carriage. No, tiaras stay on our heads and do not fit well up our noses. Remember, you are a lovely flower, and lovely flowers don't bite each other!" all the while trying not to miss my cues.

At one point there was a set piece that had to be slid on stage, a task easily performed even with my leash. I was rapidly moving towards the edge of the stage when I suddenly felt myself being tugged rather sharply backwards.

Six little pumpkins had decided to take out their boredom by turning me into "Backstage Crew Member the Ride," letting me drag them across the floor. Clinging to my electronic leash like rats onto the ropes of a sinking ship, I found myself stopped about a yard short of my goal, not wanting to pull any harder because those headsets cost more than my car insurance for a year.

I called a "Mayday! Mayday!" over the headset and punted the set piece on stage. Luckily no one seemed to notice that the set piece bounced on stage nearly hitting Cinderella in the leg. I spent the next ten minutes trying to disentangle my cord from several pairs of little hands.

Meanwhile, on the other side of the stage, Karissa, who is one of the most precocious people I have ever met, was managing to keep her throng of little ones entertained and quiet as I was trying to get back to my post without stepping on a tutu clad child.

During this same act I had to move out a fireplace on wheels, several chairs and a giant pillar, all the while trying not to kick a flower with my work boots.

As the story on stage developed, the little ones became more and more energetic. It was as if plot advancement was cocaine for these kids. Finally, there came a scene in which all of the little girls dressed like pumpkins and flowers, which were approximately three quarters of the brood, were to be on stage.

Sighing with some relief I checked in on the rest of the crew, some of whom wondered why the fireplace had peeked out on stage three scenes early. While I tried to explain that some of the girls wanted to use it as a battering ram, I watched the little tykes on stage.

The tiny ones remained calm and as professional as three or four year olds can be, except for one little pumpkin. This little pumpkin had had some issues during the practice trying to figure out which set of spike tape on the stage was hers.

After repeating where she was to stand and dance more times than there are swear words in *The Blues Brothers* she had finally learned where *her* spot was. Due to the girls being three and four years old, however, the girl next to her during the performance got confused and accidentally moved over onto this girl's stage markings.

This was an insult to our little pumpkin worse than the peacetime bombing of a civilian target. The diminutive vegetable continued to dance, but she glared at the girl next to her, her eyes filling to the brim with rage.

During the song, there was a part where the Fairy Godmother, in all her glittering Glinda-esque glory, was to hand out wands to the little girls for the second half of the number. As she bestowed the glimmering plastic props, every little girl took hers and gracefully curtsied, returning to her place on the stage.

Every little girl, that is, except the perturbed pumpkin, who stomped up to the Fairy Godmother, snatched the wand and stomped back to the place next to the girl who had taken her spot.

Karissa and I watched from the wings as the little girls went back to slowly twirling in semi-unison on stage. The piece was coming to an end, when suddenly the defiant dancer struck.

I was in the middle of getting instructions from the booth when abruptly all conversation stopped as the little girl on stage suddenly reached out with her wand and smacked the flower in the face.

The other little girl, too shocked to scream, stood motionless as the song ended, the victorious pumpkin holding her wand above her head as she twirled prettily until the curtain closed.

It's a good thing one of the other older ballerinas was there to comfort the now crying victim, because I was too busy laughing and Karissa was too preoccupied saying, "Wait, what just happened!?"

The show plowed on, the crew and I resorting to limericks and old jokes just to stay conscious as Karissa and I attempted to keep the little ones from chewing on something dangerous. At last, one of the ending numbers came up, and every little ballerina was needed on stage.

The stage filled with little pumpkins, flowers and Funfetti cupcakes, which we later were told were jesters, who danced awkwardly, but prettily. Now, the game plan after this number was that the little girls would split into two groups, and calmly proceed offstage on either side.

The song ended, the girls stood confused, a little tired and dazed. All of them stood there, knowing that something was supposed to happen, something important. Suddenly, as if by some simultaneous mental transmission, the little girls remembered they were supposed to be off stage some ten seconds earlier.

If you've never had the chance to participate in the running of the bulls, then might I suggest volunteering to work backstage at a ballet that features over forty little ballerinas, it's a similar experience. The little girls all turned in near unison, faced me, and charged.

My coworkers tell me that all they could hear over the headset was, "Holy Funfetti cupcakes!!!!!" and the sounds of thudding little feet as every single little girl ran towards me in a mad rush to get out of the stage lights.

Needless to say I had very colorful nightmares for weeks afterwards.

So what granules of help can be extracted from the sugar bowl of information?

1. Just because it's cute and dressed in a tutu does not mean that it isn't a vicious creature that might try to strangle you with your work equipment.

2. A fake pumpkin carriage prop can hold the weight of approximately five or six small children.

3. Victory will be yours if you are a pumpkin carrying a wand.

32. PEZ AND WORLD DOMINATION

I'm not really an out of the box thinker. No instead I prefer to sit in the box, and make it into a spaceship and then fly it to wherever I need to go.

I have discovered incredible uses for perfectly mundane or bizarre items. This is due in part to the fact that I have propensity to fiddle with just about everything in my environment, and the fact that I wanted to be an evil scientist when I was a kid. Unfortunately I barely passed chemistry in high school, so evil scientist-hood was never to be mine. What remnants of that dream have remained though have made me into an improviser of epic proportions.

In my travels across this planet I have found a tool that is so universal it puts MacGyver's bomb made from toothpicks and half a stick of masticated gum to the test; a Santa Claus PEZ dispenser.

At one point I worked for a charitable organization that did outreach to homeless and at-risk youth in Spokane, Washington. This was perhaps the best job I could have ever fathomed, not only because it was challenging and emotionally rewarding, but because it regularly gave me some of the weirdest sets of circumstances I could have imagined.

We were mostly supported via donations from the community. For the most part the donations were useful things like socks, granola bars and deodorant, things that made life a little more bearable on the cold streets during winter. Other donations made us wonder if the donor had decided to make their gift after about ten gin and tonics (heavy on the gin).

It was around Christmas time that we found ourselves bestowed with a gift that was about as useful to street kids as a Winnebago is to a sperm whale; about 150 Santa Claus PEZ dispensers. In the words of the outreach team's fearless leader, Kari, "This makes sense, because gang bangers love Santa!?"

We spent the week leading up to Christmas trying to farm out the dumb plastic items to as many kids as we could. It got to the point where we only gave out the other supplies we carried with us if we could also give the befuddled teenager a candy-dispensing piece of crap. If you've never had the chance to give a hard-core street-entrenched gang-banger a small bright colored candy dispenser, then let me tell you, there is nothing like that look of holiday confusion on their face.

While these things were almost of no use to us on the streets, though, I began to find other uses for them.

The first time that winter I found myself in dire need of a Santa Claus PEZ dispenser I had just completed the second half of the caffeine delivery system. I went to flush the toilet in my apartment only to hear a resounding "plunk!" reminiscent of one losing their olive in their martini.

Removing the back of the toilet tank revealed that the "chain" to my toilet had broken.

I say "chain," using the condescending quotation marks, because the developmentally disabled gorilla that had installed my apartment toilet had installed a plug that was not attached to the handle by an actual chain. Instead they had used a thin strip of plastic that was weakly molded between the two necessary parts. This meant a simple fix involving a paper-clip was out of the question.

I searched my apartment for a tool I could use to lift the plug in my toilet tank; all of my hangers were the thick plastic useless types, I didn't want to use my silverware, and I didn't have any recent exes who had left anything at my place that I wouldn't mind sticking in a toilet tank. Then the thought struck me, several of those damn PEZ dispensers had made it home with me in my workbag.

I picked up the phone and dialed my boss' phone number. Kari picked up the phone as I just blurted out, "Can I use one of the donated PEZ thingamajiggers for a non-work-related task?"

Kari, having experienced the way my brain works before, sighed and asked suspiciously, "Whyyyyyyy?"

"Umm... do you really want to know?"

"Yes, Allison, I really do."

I paused as I tried to come up with some delicate way to explain my predicament. After a few seconds I realized that trying to put the task at hand lightly was kind of like trying to explain deep existential philosophy via pantomime.

It was my turn to sigh, "There is no good way to put this, I need to use one to flush my damn toilet."

"Whaaaaaat?"

I rapidly explained the situation and my planned use for the festive piece of plastic, which had a very handy little hook-like edge at the bottom that fit nicely under the edge of my toilet plug. I finished elucidating my situation only to hear silence on the other end. Suddenly, Kari exploded into laughter that lasted long enough to teach a penguin how to make brownies.

When she finally regained her ability to make human language sounds again, she sputtered out, "Yes, as long as you promise to take pictures. I need to see this!"

That PEZ dispenser flushed my toilet for almost two weeks until my landlady finally came to fix the problem.

Not two or three days later I found another fantastic use for our seemingly useless Christmas reminders. The outreach team I worked with operated out of a downtown teen youth shelter, which the drug dealers, for the most part, knew to stay away from.

However, there was this one dope dealing doofus who decided to set up shop right outside the shelter. This was the same idiot that had been selling product out of a clear plastic Subway bag right across the street from the shelter a couple weeks before. He was so surprised when the cops picked him up.

Apparently, right after getting out of jail, he had decided to try selling at a different spot where he was sure the cops wouldn't catch him; right in front of the shelter staffed with the people who had reported him the first time he got arrested.

Noticing he was outside one of the shelter staff went out and told him sternly to leave. He wandered away from the front door for about a yard and a half and then stopped again.

Kari rolled her eyes, went outside and told him to move his ass. Trudging back indoors she got to watch as he proceeded to move another yard and a half as he stopped again. At this point we were all pretty peeved with this idiot's presence, so I decided to take matters into my own hands.

Grabbing a PEZ dispenser like Xena might grab her sword, I walked outside and yelled, "Go the hell away!" as I threw the PEZ dispenser at the guy.

Confused, he watched as a flying Santa whisked past his head. He left.

I walked back indoors where Kari wide-eyed said, "You probably shouldn't have done that."

I shrugged, "I was giving him a gift, my method of delivery was just a little confusing."

Probably the best use for a PEZ dispenser came to me when I ended up working on a Saturday. A local environmental concerns group, in an act of great charity, had decided to host a breakfast for the homeless. As they did not normally work with this population they had sent a request to my employers to send someone with a little more experience to help out. Guess who the lucky emissary was?

I walked into the rather nice lobby of this company's building dressed in my street clothes of ratty jeans, an old t-shirt, a sweatshirt and an utter lack of make-up to top the look off. I was met by a group of perky looking volunteers dressed in polo shirts, suits and shoes that probably cost more than my car insurance for a year. I actually asked one of the volunteers if they realized that the homeless didn't tend to come to "black tie only" events, right?

As the people came in off the streets into the plush lobby of this marble tiled building to eat a warm meal, it was apparent that there was going to be a culture clash about as dramatic as introducing medieval knights to a group of preppy fraternity brothers.

Everything went smoothly enough for about the first half hour. Then a guy came in, obviously higher than the Hubble Telescope. He walked up to a lady volunteer, got about two inches away from her face and said, rather loudly, "Your eyeballs, I like them, they look tasty..." The volunteers looked absolutely horrified as I burst into raucous laughter.

I led the wide-eyed tweaker through the food line and got him sat down, where he stayed for approximately a second. I spent the next fifteen minutes attempting to herd this guy towards a seat instead of trying to climb up the stairway railing. Suddenly, I remembered that I had my workbag with me, and that I still had a PEZ dispenser left. I grabbed the Santa and handed it to the man whose attention span was shorter than a dachshund puppy.

The man's eyes widened to the point where I was slightly concerned his eyes might actually fall out. He took the PEZ dispenser held it above his head like angels had just delivered it to him from heaven. Then he looked at me and said, "Thank you, High Priestess Daughter of the Gods!"

Then he ran out the door, candy contraption still above his head, making whooshing noises like a kid playing Superman.

I would like that title on my resume or at least on a t-shirt. Regardless, these experiences have taught me some very important lessons:

1. A PEZ dispenser is just as vital to a person's functional survival as a Swiss Army Knife, duct tape or rope.

2. If you need to dispose of a drug dealer, the Christmas Spirit can be used as a weapon.

3. Your boss will not allow you to add a nameplate that reads "High Priestess Daughter of the Gods" to your desk, no matter how much it is true.

33. IT'S RAINING JERKS, HALLELUJAH?

I have a tactic for turning down dates from creepers; I call it the Confuse and Conquer. Much as a military general forces his troops to crawl around in the mud to practice being miserable and avoiding the enemy, I have sent my mind and verbiage through a similar boot camp.

Basically the C and C tactic requires one to say something that will take the other person the same amount of time it takes for one to make a paper hat for a flamingo to figure out exactly what your answer was.

"Hey, you wanna go out sometime?" some creepy guy in line at the supermarket will ask.

"I'm sorry, my religion prohibits me from going on a date with anyone I just met on any day that ends in y."

By the time the line creeper has figured out that means, "Oh hell no!" I have bagged my groceries and escaped.

"When are you next free to go out?" asks the ex who just won't leave you alone.

"Janfebmarch," I say as I skitter to safety.

"Do you want to go out this Friday?" says the coworker you have already nicely turned down five or six times.

"Sorry, that's my night to walk the goldfish," I mutter as I busy myself with any mundane task I can find.

I have discovered this tactic has about an 86% success rate. The exceptions to the rule are the people don't actually listen to what you say, those who actually have enough intact brain cells to figure it out before you can make a Scooby-Doo style getaway or the extremely persistent shit-twinkle.

The last option is always the worst to try and get rid of. Like a koala on its home tree, trying to get the persistent ones to leave you alone is a task best handled by a baseball bat to a kneecap. If you don't want to go to prison, however, then one will have to turn to less violent tactics.

One such barnacle of desired relationship was a friend of a friend who we will call Bubba. To say that Bubba was a little tenacious is kind of like saying Paula Deen likes butter just a little. I literally turned down his advances so many times that I eventually just greeted him with, "No."

Of course, you might ask, "What was so wrong with Bubba?"

Let's try the fact that the first time he met me he went for a boob grab, or the fact that he talked about his other sexual exploits constantly or the fact that I just didn't like his face.

Not to be thwarted by my constant eye-rolls and refusals, he came to a game night hosted by a mutual friend. We were all hanging out, playing board games until all hours, because that's what poor people who can't afford to do more fascinating things do, when he strode in, eyeing me like I was the last crab-leg at the buffet.

Throughout the evening Bubba continued to follow me around the room. I'd move to a chair, he'd tip the person in the chair next to me out of it so he could sit there. I'd move to the floor, he'd move the chair behind me. I'd move so that my back was to a wall and he'd find some way to squeeze in next to me.

This went on until around 3 in the morning. Now I will admit, when I get tired, I tend to get a bit bitchy. At this juncture, though, I'd had enough. There was nothing I could do, say, or hint at that would make this guy leave me alone. I couldn't knock him unconscious and throw him out the window, because he was still the friend of my friend.

It was at this desperate hour that he moved in on the couch next to me, trying to put his arm around me, and I panicked. Much like the rat loses its tail when threatened by a predator, I dropped all sense of dignity and let rip the gnarliest fart I could manage.

This is something I *never* do in public. Hell, I try not to even burp in public, but with the incoming douchebag imminent it was the only option my tired brain could think up.

There was silence in the room for a second before one of the other people said, "Did you just use gas as a defense mechanism against Bubba?"

Angrily glaring at the now backed off idiot, I nodded. Those gathered applauded.

A week later the same friend and I were spending an evening out on the town and we stopped into a club that had a dance floor because it sounded like fun to make fools out of ourselves. I don't dance, I twitch awkwardly in rhythm with music. I have Caucasian Rhythm Disorder and it shows.

This and the fact that I don't really go to clubs to try to pick people up, means that my ideal partner is a single gay man.

Gay men are the best dance partners at clubs ever; they won't try to grab you inappropriately, they don't care if you dance like an idiot and they are often the sweetest people on the planet ever. After all gay means happy, right?

I quickly made friends with a tall, red-bearded man who kept calling me, "Daaaarling." He had just broken up with his boyfriend and was out just to have fun. Perfect.

We danced together for a while, just having fun, neither of us really paying attention to what was going on around us. The lack of my usual super-vigilance, however, came back to bite me in the butt like an urban legend alligator in a toilet.

As we danced around on the dance floor I suddenly found my "douche-dar" going off at epic levels. My Spi-the-jerk Sense was not wrong, as I turned around to find myself almost toe to toe with Bubba.

I believe my exact reaction was, "What the glerk!?"

At that point, because I had no intention of giving this guy any more seconds of my life I, as my grandmother would put it, skedaddled. I quickly thanked my new tall red-bearded friend for the dance, and got out of the building like it was being attacked by Elvis impersonators armed with rubber mallets.

What happened next was later related to me by friends who had remained in the club. Apparently no sooner than I had made a hasty escape, Bubba had started into a tirade to anyone who would listen about how much of a "prudish bitch" I was because I would not sleep with him. He ranted, attempting to be heard over the din of the club, calling me every name that a woman can be called for approximately ten seconds.

Don't get me wrong, Bubba would have ranted until the skies turned to Jell-O, he just suddenly found himself incapable of doing so. Mid-insult the very tall, very buff, gay man I had been dancing with said, "Don't you *dare* talk about her like that, you little pussy!" and body checked Bubba with enough force to send him flying over a table.

I'm told Bubba regained his feet and tried to save face by throwing out some very not-nice words for those of alternate orientation. Those, however, were drowned out by a very determined hand, attached to a very solid body, which was attached to a very loud voice that boomed, "You don't get to call her *any* of that, she was gorgeous and totally sweet, and you're a prick who just needs to leave her alone!"

Bubba avoided me after that. I never saw my brave defender again, but sir, wherever you are, I owe you a hug.

So what lessons can be swooped across the dance floor of experience?

1. If you can't tell them no with words, telling them no with uncommon bodily sounds and smells might be a better option.

2. Chivalry isn't dead, it sometimes just takes finding a man who has better taste in shoes than you do to prove it.

34. DANCE LIKE EVERYONE IS WATCHING

Uma Thurman has been credited with saying, "Boredom is the mother of invention."

We should not only listen to her because she is an incredible actress and can pull off a white, stretchy, dress phenomenally, but because she is right. However, I would like to add that not only does boredom breed innovation, it can also be the harbinger of disaster.

I don't sit still well. I'm kind of a ball of muscle bound energy, and even as I type this I am using my foot to tease a kitten. So putting me in one spot for long periods of time works about as well as trying to contain a wolverine on Red Bull inside a cardboard box.

At one time, a job I had involved traveling around and giving short presentations on a service the group I worked for had to offer. These were presentations aimed at local businesses in the hopes of getting them to jump on the bandwagon and support the community initiative my employers were putting forth.

This meant I got dressed up in a suit, did my little Vanna White shtick and then high-tailed it to the next place all the while praying that everyone was running on time.

The day in question had been a long day. I had given 6 or 7 of these presentations, and the last group I was supposed to speak to was a counseling firm with a staff of more than 30 people. The head counselor there had requested I come in and speak during their staff meeting so that everyone could be present.

I showed up at my allotted time, and was told by the receptionist that things were running a little behind and that if I wanted to sit in the room right outside the conference room, they'd call me in in a few minutes. I stood in the lobby, staring into nothing, because that was what this room was: A white little box of nothing.

An overhead speaker blared out some salsa music, and I started to tap my foot to the beat. The room literally had no decorations and one, very uncomfortable looking, chair. The minutes dragged by.

After 5 minutes, my foot tap turned into a hip wiggle.

After 10 minutes, the hip wiggle turned into some small dance steps.

After 20 minutes, I had given up at containing myself and was full-blown dancing in this tiny waiting area.

Now, I must explain, I don't dance. I have a tendency to waltz like one of my legs is shorter than the other, turn a tango into a new sport that involves tackling and somehow make hip-hop look like a full body dry heave. I have had one salsa dancing lesson in which the instructor suggested, "I spend my time doing other things." So, whatever I was doing in the waiting area, was probably not something graceful, rhythmic or even remotely artistic.

The door finally opened, and I immediately stopped, straightened my suit jacket and put on an air of sophistication and poise. I then stared confusedly at the man, who was red-faced with tears streaming down his cheeks as he half-said half-choked out, "We're ready for you now."

I entered the room to find the entire staff assembled, all looking quite a bit like the man who had come to retrieve me. The room had two TV's mounted to the walls, and the content of the screen looked very familiar.

Then it hit me, the tiny little waiting area had a security camera, and I had just done a one-man show for over 10 minutes set to crappy elevator salsa music. I looked at the screens for a beat, then looked back to the room full of strangers who had just gotten their own personal show, and bowed. The room erupted into applause.

So what slivers of knowledge can be tweezed from the finger of stupidity?

1. Never assume you're alone. This may sound paranoid, but if paranoia saves you from utter embarrassment, then be as paranoid as you like. Wear a tin-foil hat if it helps.

2. If you're going to fail, at least do so in a way that makes 30 other peoples' meeting that much more entertaining.

35. NO, JUST NO

In my dating life I have had several one hit wonders; as in, I dated them once, and then wondered why I dated them. Having dated everything from the guy who, after anytime I made a snarky comment, said, "That's funny, and it's funny because..." to the one who complained that our shoes didn't match, I can officially say that I have about as much luck in dating as a person who walks under a ladder, while kicking a black cat and smashing 13 mirrors as they go.

The one that tops the list of terrible will never-date-agains has to be a guy who we will, to protect what remains of his ego, as Bud.

Bud was a man's man, he liked biking, and hiking, and camping in the woods in the middle of winter just to prove he did not fear cold!!!

That and the fact that he had one of the most impressive... music collections (what were you thinking, you horrible person, you?), meant that I conceded to go on a date one October evening with Bud.

At this point I was in college in dinky little Nampa, Idaho (population 30 people, 4 million cows). What does one do in October in Nampa, aside from cry miserably that you did not choose somewhere warmer to receive an education? One goes to corn mazes, and if one is feeling extra fancy, one goes to a *haunted* corn maze.

Let me be absolutely clear on one subject, I find horror movies rather hilarious. I have yet to watch a flick from that genre that has made me more frightened than I would be over someone's puppy stuffed animal. *The Ring, Saw, Paranormal Activity*, none had an effect on me. So the idea of going to a "haunted" corn maze, sounded fun on the same level as getting into a marshmallow throwing war might be.

The haunted corn maze in Nampa is mostly staffed by teenagers trying to make a few extra bucks by dressing up in terrible costumes and jumping out of exceedingly obvious hiding places in an effort to startle the living daylights out of whoever they can. However, if you get lost a werewolf or Frankenstein's monster will kindly direct you towards which way you should go.

The most frightening part of the maze is realizing that you have to pee 15 minutes into a 3-hour long hike through mud and dried out rows of corn.

The night we went to the corn maze, Bud and I saw several of our friends going in ahead of us. We jovially said, "hello," and were not terribly surprised to see familiar faces since this was the only new and mildly entertaining thing to do for miles around. They went in ahead of us, and a few minutes later we entered, my date intrepidly in the lead.

We wandered past some creepily hung giant cobwebs, which may or may not have at one point been some little old lady's doily collection, and turned a corner by a coffin. I was beginning to wonder if our high school attackers had fallen asleep amongst the corn when suddenly a werewolf sprung from behind a clump of corn.

Now, when I say "werewolf" I'm not talking a furry beast with blood dripping from its menacing fangs as it howls at the moon. What I mean by "werewolf" is a gangly teenager, with a fake beard and some fake bushy eyebrows who nearly tripped on the corn he was jumping from behind as he confusedly said, "Roar?"

Bud, in an act of true masculine heroism only paralleled by Captain America, Superman and Thor all rolled into one, proceeded to jump behind me while yelling, "No. take the girl!"

Be still my beating heart, my hero is here to save me.

We spent the rest of the maze with me, walking like a normal human being, and my date clinging to me like a koala bear on steroids as he hid behind me and whimpered.

When we reached the other side of the maze, not only had I lost all feeling in my left arm, but I was met with the puzzled expressions of our friends who had finished the maze a little before us.

One of my good friends turned to me, with an expression that denoted she had just been shown a picture of a kangaroo holding an Uzi and said, "Allison, I have *never* heard you scream that loud before, ever."

I simply shook my head and glanced over at Bud who was still hunkered down behind me with his eyes closed, possibly saying the Lord's Prayer underneath his breath. Her face took on a new expression, one that spoke volumes of pity as she simply uttered, "Oh, umm... is your arm purple?"

What fleas of knowledge can be picked from the coat of experience?

111

1. No matter what excuse you come up with later, offering your date as a sacrifice at the first sign of a teenager wrapped in toilet paper who mumbles, "boo," is not going to land you a second date.

2. The ringing in your ears caused by nearly constant screaming will eventually go away, it might just take a year or three.

3. It is fair to ask potential dates if they have ever been scared by a stuffed CareBear before.

36. ADVENTURES OF THE NAKED NINJA

My mother has held many careers in her lifetime. She has been a rock-radio disc jockey, stand-in musician for various bands, a newswoman, horse trainer, bank teller, interior designer... the list goes on like a kleptomaniac's rap-sheet. However, her fallback job, when she's in between the thing she used to want to do and the thing she now wants to do, has always been teaching piano lessons.

This means that I spent many years completely used to the fact that random strangers would be wandering through our house. I grew extremely comfortable with this, to the point where wandering to the kitchen, which was located near the room my mother taught piano lessons, to pour myself a bowl of cereal wearing Batman boxers became second nature to me.

For the most part my mother's students were little kids, whose parents were doing what any good parent would do and force their child into after-school activities, or middle-aged persons having a mid-life crisis and realizing that their parents spent hundreds of dollars on piano lessons when they were younger that they never used. Neither of these groups really inspired me to look my best when wandering about the house.

All that changed with one student, who for embarrassment purposes we will name "Studly." I was about fifteen when Studly started taking piano lessons from my mother. Studly was tall, Greek and handsome. In his late teens, Studly was not only extremely easy on the eyes, but was the lead singer in a metal band.

At fifteen one does not think about things like, "Does he have a good credit score?" or "Is his band actually any good?" (the answer to that sadly being no), instead one thinks thoughts like, "He plays guitar and he smells like he showers more than once a week!"

I did my best to look like I actually gave a damn whenever I knew his lesson was coming up. Of course, at fifteen for me this meant wearing a t-shirt with no holes in it and remembering to wear a little bit of make-up (take note parents, that's what you get when you raise a punk).

At one point my mother decided that she wanted to paint her kitchen gold. Now by, "wanted to paint her kitchen" I actually mean, "she wanted her kitchen to magically change colors without her ever having to touch a brush."

So, being the savvy person that she was, she decided to trade Studly some piano lessons to climb up on a ladder for an evening and paint.

I was not really given prior warning that this was happening, for the most part my mother and I never really communicated the daily goings on of each other's lives. So it was a little bit of a surprise when I was in the garage using our old trusty stationary bike to work out, and my mom pulled in with the car and said, "Oh by the way, Studly is going to be here in five minutes."

I froze for a second, dripping from the sweat of over an hour spent biking like I was being chased by the stationary hounds of hell. Then I was gone in a cartoonish puff of smoke. Throwing my clothes off as if they had been infested with sand crabs I made a break for the shower in my mom's master bathroom because it was farther back in the house. Only halfway through my shower did it dawn on me that I should probably have brought clean clothes into the bathroom with me.

I clambered out of the shower to hear my mother's voice in her bedroom. Hoping to get a little assistance I threw the door open halfway and quickly slammed it shut again. Mom was giving Studly a guided tour of the house. At the slamming door I heard Studly ask, "What was that!?"

"Just the sound of embarrassment," my mother calmly replied.

My mother continued on with her tour as if her butt-naked daughter wasn't standing mortified in the bathroom. I waited the amount of time it would take for settlers to cross the Oregon Trail using legless oxen before I cautiously opened the door again. Clutching the only towel I could find, a hand towel, around myself as best I could I made a break for my bedroom.

I dove with Mission Impossible determination into my room and slammed the door shut with enough force to cause the house to rattle. My most sneaky and smooth move ever, let me tell you.

I dashed over to my closet, quickly found a cute shirt and then went for pants, only to then discover that karma is a bitch. As it turns out, if you forget to do your laundry for a week there is no magical laundry fairy that will sense impending pantsless doom and wash all of your pants for you.

I stood, staring at my closet and blinking, as if that particular action would suddenly produce pants that were not sitting in a laundry basket in a different part of the house. It was at this point that I heard my mother call, "Hey, dinner's here for the eating!"

The only thing that I had that was clean and not full of holes was a pair of AC/DC pajama pants, and let me tell you pajama pants that are three sizes too big, woah momma, that shit is hot!

It was at this point that I strongly contemplated bailing out the window. I actually called one of my friends to see if she was free at that point to drive over and save my mortified hide. She didn't answer her phone.

Resigning myself to the fact that there was no way in Satan skiing on a pile of skulls Hell that I was going to be able to escape or hide my white-trash background, I marched out towards the dining area. On my way there I went through the five stages of grief over my less than stellar appearance before the king of Mt. Olympus; denial, anger, shiny object, forgetting why I was upset to begin with and trying to figure out how peanut butter is made.

By the time I walked into the kitchen-dining area I basically decided, "So what I'm wearing AC/DC pajama pants!? So what I just dove my naked butt across a hallway and into a bedroom with him no more than a slingshot's shooting distance away!? So wha—"

My bad-ass self-confidence musings were rudely interrupted as my tiny version of a dog Paddy-Wak darted in front of me and I face planted directly at Studly's feet.

I just stayed there for a moment, face smooshed into the linoleum, like an unlucky ant underneath the tire of a moped, contemplating where my life had gone wrong. Deciding it had gone wrong sometime around my second day out of the womb, I began to peel myself off the floor.

Studly, being the awesome gentleman that partially earned him his nickname here, offered me a hand. I got up, holding onto my pajama pants in case they became prey to a sudden gravity storm, winced, and said the oh so gracious and charming, "How's it going dude?"

Needless to say, this Disney-esque fairytale did not end with me marrying the handsome prince, but it did lend me some important lessons.

1. Sometimes it would pay to constantly walk around looking like a fashion model. However, why spend all that effort when you could learn a new skill instead, like knife throwing.

2. This is perhaps why I've spent a lot of time single.

3. There is no substitution for a sense of humor and misplaced confidence, unless that substitution happens to be an entire beauty team that can magically spring from your bedroom closet of course.

37. SQUISH

High class as I am, I tend to find myself in a lot of situations that absolutely reek of fine champagne, fine silver and bottles of water that cost upwards of $5.00.

Ok, that is a bold faced lie. I tend to behave badly in "high class" situations, mostly because if I gave any more craps about acting perfectly prim and proper, then more important things, like not killing people with a shovel, would go crapless.

As such, one is far more likely to find me playing darts in a hole in the wall bar against a tattooed biker than they are attempting to waltz with Prince Charming.

It stands to reason then, that if you give me an opportunity to go do something completely undignified and possibly including violence I will be there immediately. This is the appeal of mosh-pits for me.

Yes, at 5'3" mosh-pits basically mean playing a giant game of "dodge the elbows," but regardless, I love throwing myself into a group of people and being tossed around a bit. Plus, if the band is terrible, then one can easily escape the awful music.

One such concert I attended was the trifecta of perfect mosh-pit setting; it was outdoors on a summer day, there were over 1,000 people in attendance and the band truly sucked more than an industrial strength vacuum cleaner.

The only downside was the fact that on either side of me were two girls who I will call Mosh-pit Stupid. These are the people who go in wearing a white, thin t-shirt and ironic glasses and who come out with the bloody scraps of what used to be a shirt and the inability to see anything. These two girls on the stupid scale of one to spends a lot of time trying to read bricks, were right around the attempting to breathe steel wool level of dumb.

Both girls were sporting bikini tops, Daisy Duke shorts that were threatening to disappear up their butt-cracks, flip-flops and enough make-up that they could probably face-plant off of the Empire State Building and survive. Both of them used me, as I could easily fit both of their double zero sized waists behind me, as an impromptu shield on several occasions as I was busily trying to avoid getting my face smashed in by some inebriated rivet-head.

There are very few rules in a mosh-pit, but there are a few unspoken ones that everyone who dares to enter a flying group of bodies should respect. The first is never drag someone from outside the mosh-pit into it, mostly because if that person happens to be carrying beer then you will spill it and that would be a crying shame. The second is if at first the mosh-pit refuses to crowd surf you because you weigh more than all of the Thunder Cats combined, don't continue to try.

Of course there are those who believe the unspoken rules of nature do not apply to them. These people brazenly laugh in the face of the roaring lion, promptly before the lion eats one of their limbs. One such individual was at this concert.

Weighing at approximately 350 pounds of pure living in your parents' basement laziness, this fine paragon of society decided to crowd surf. I watched as he went up, and then crashed down to earth like a meteor made of Donald Trump's hair pieces. Then again as he went up, only to find out again that gravity sucks.

Frustrated with his lack of anti-terra firma defying ways, he decided to start with a more bulky, robust group of men about three people over from where I was existing. He went up, he got shoved my direction, and the girls on either side of me stepped out and away on either side.

Do you remember watching cartoons in which Wile E. Coyote gets a huge boulder dropped on his head? He broke the fourth wall, looked to the audience for help as his knees shook, then the boulder would unceremoniously crush him. That is exactly what happened, except I did not get up in some form of comical accordion spring-like fashion.

No instead I got up only after the guy realized that he was lying on top of someone. I actually remember a bystander saying, "Holy shit, there was actually a person under there!" I literally saw stars for three and a half hours afterwards.

So what lessons can we check off of our list of things to learn?

1. Mosh pits are not for frail things. If you, yourself, are a frail thing, don't go into a mosh pit, because more likely than not you will get someone else injured. That someone will most likely be me.

2. There are some dreams that can never be reached. I will never be an Olympic gymnast or a professional food taster. If you weigh more than all of the furniture in my apartment put together, then crowd surfing is a dream you should probably set aside for more useful ideas.

38. LET'S TAKE SALVATION AWAY FROM HERE

In my experience there are two kinds of missionary workers/evangelicals/street preachers. The first is a well-balanced person who realizes that before one can tend to the soul of a person, one must gain their trust and meet their basic needs. The second, is like a giant golden retriever puppy: it's so excited you can't understand what it wants and it may end up peeing on itself out of sheer exuberant joy.

The first one can calmly hear, "Why no, I don't feel like accepting *insert religion* today," and they will wish you luck and send you on your way. The second will take your negative answer and respond by cramming holy pamphlets, or sometimes religiously-themed comic books, into your hand while screaming, "REPENT!" at decibels that I'm sure shake the ground on Mount Olympus.

Now, and I say this as a Christian, but it seems that the two religious groups most likely to be in the second category are Christians and Mormons. Before we get a lot of angry letters telling my editor that I should be burned at the stake, and then eaten like steak, I have a lot of friends of both religions, and I admire aspects of both. Christians know how to get a yard-sale together like nobody's business and Mormons have the best potlucks hands down.

However, when you read in the news that either of these groups oppose something, it is very rarely followed by the words, "peacefully," "logically," and "civilly." This is perhaps due to the media's need to sensationalize everything. I maintain, however, that it's just the loudest and most obnoxious of any group that makes it on T.V.

When there is a natural disaster in any part of the country they never interview a doctor or a college professor. No, instead the media finds the loudest, most tooth-deprived soul they can drum up and sticks a camera in their face just long enough for them to say something like, "Well, I'll be deep fried! That was the most damn-blasted storm I ever did see! I looked out my window to see the trailer next door get picked up off the ground and all I could think is, 'Well, guess my wash on the line is a goner!'"

The sad thing is, that even if it is the nut-jobs from any group that the media focuses on, these crazy singularly focused people still exist in the real world.

Case in point came when I was working as a homeless and at-risk youth outreach worker in downtown Spokane. In this job, which I spent mostly wandering around trying to convince my clients to take the condoms off of their heads and go to their court appointments, I ran into a lot of the local color.

One day, as a coworker and I were walking looking for our elusive clients, we suddenly saw a group of them scatter and run like a herd of bemused wildebeests that someone had started an air-raid siren in the middle of.

Very few things will make a group of street-kids panic and run; Truancy Officers, Police Officers who hold active arrest warrants, clowns with balloon animals... So as my coworker and I approached we peered cautiously at what we might be faced with. It was worse than all those options put together, it was street missionaries.

Now, I won't tell you what group these specific suit and tie clad young men were from as to protect their anonymity. Let us just say that if you rearranged their religion's acronym you could make LSD. These two smartly dressed individuals promptly locked their targets on us and made a beeline for the only thing not running for blocks around.

"Would you like to hear about---"

"Nope!" My coworker interjected before a spiel could be started.

However, by then it was already too late, and we were both subjected to a 20-minute lecture on how our souls needed to be saved right then, there and now!

You might ask why we did not try to escape. We did. Unfortunately, each and every time we tried to explain that we had street children we needed to find and throw fruit snacks at, we were handed pamphlets. By the end of their speech, we each had enough pamphlets to explain who is responsible for the rainforests disappearing.

Trying anything to escape having our souls saved, my coworker and I turned the conversation onto the two subjects that will distract ninety-five percent of the population; we talked to the two missionaries about themselves. We found out that these two young, clean cut, had probably never been within 20 yards of a bar young men were from some dinky town in Utah. They were so excited to be in the "big city" they could hardly contain themselves.

Now Spokane is relatively large, it is the second largest city in Washington state, but my coworker had lived in Boston, Massachusetts and I had lived in Atlanta, Georgia, so we found this a tad funny. They prattled on about how this was their first experience out on the street, and we nodded, half paying attention and half looking for an escape route.

Finally my coworker and I were able to extract ourselves, wishing that we had taken a leaf from our kids' book and had dashed away like hamsters on Pixie Stix at the first sign of suits and greased down hair. Leaving with our pile of what would eventually become doodle paper, we went in search of our scattered clients.

About half an hour we had moved to a part of downtown where people don't lock their cars. This isn't because it's a trusting, safe, happy place. People don't lock their car doors because they would rather the hoodlums breaking into their vehicle didn't smash a window to do so.

Surrounded by gang tags, alleys that looked like some post-apocalyptic scenery and about three drug deals, my coworker and I felt right at home. This is what we did on a daily basis, and so nothing we saw was really remotely shocking to us. Something that day seemed a bit off, and knowing our "we would prefer to go home bullet free tonight" limits, we proceeded with caution.

We peered around until we spotted what was making our Spidey-senses tingle. There was a group of gang bangers, mostly armed to the teeth, arms crossed, with looks that said, "Someone's about to get cut," on each of their faces.

Then we saw it. Smack dab in the middle of what was probably collectively 90 years of already served prison time, was our two gung-ho missionaries, waving pamphlets around.

My coworker and I stood, absolutely shocked, for a minute before she chimed in with, "Well, we should probably save them."

"Who, the missionaries or the gang bangers?"

For once some of the more entrenched gang members looked happy to see us as we sauntered up. The gang bangers didn't want to have to kill these idiots, their bodies would be kind of hard to hide in the middle of a Tuesday afternoon.

We smiled at the armed Crips surrounding us, grabbed the missionaries and said, "Hey, we need to be saved. No really, we need to be saved right freakin' now!"

My coworker and I dragged the extremely excited missionaries over to the other side of the road, one of whom actually said, "Yay, our first converts!"

I sighed deeply and pointed to the still staring gang bangers, "Do you see that group of people?"

"Yes."

"Do you know why they are all dressed in blue?"

"No."

"Honey, those are gang bangers."

Both missionaries stared at me, "Yes, you have wandered into their territory and they aren't a huge fan of people with pamphlets unless those pamphlets are laced with LSD."

Their eyes grew wide as I said, "You should probably reach out to people on the North side of town from now on, ok pumpkins?"

And whoosh! They were gone in a poof of hot air and pamphlets as they ran back the way they had come.

Of course, we can learn some lessons from their ill-fated sojourn into the ghetto.

1. Be aware of your surroundings. If the big angry looking men have bulges around the waistband of their pants, don't assume they are carrying large bags of candy. Those are guns and you should scamper away.

2. If you are going out to save others, please make sure that you are not putting yourself in a position where those others are actually going to have to save you.

39. SUPER SMOOTH

I am not normally one of those girls who fawns over attractive persons; batting my eyelashes and high pitch giggling are not in my repertoire. For the most part I am a confident, can have a logical conversation with a good-looking person and not drool on my shoe while doing so, type of girl.

That being said, there have been particular people I have attempted to talk to that appeared to have stolen my verbal abilities with some kind of magical mind powers.

Take for example a certain guy my freshman year of college who was smart, funny, and had biceps the size of my thigh (I'm not shallow, just ruled by my primal hormones sometimes). I had spoken to him a few times, but nothing more in depth than, "Wow, this class sucks."

I looked for an opportunity, a slight slim chance, that I might have to break the ice that stood between banal dumb comments and wonderful, might get you asked on a date, conversation. Then, as if the fates had finally decided they were done kicking me in the pancreas, someone happened to mention to me that it was his birthday. At last, I had my verbal icepick. So, in a confident and put together manner, I decided I was going to go and wish him a happy birthday.

My friend Arielle, in a display of her belief in my abilities as a courageous, strong, young, independent woman, followed me over so she could collect on her bet that I would chicken out before coming within eyesight of one of those glorious biceps.

Drunk on my own self-assurance that I could both talk and look into those blue eyes at the same time, I marched right up to where he was eating a sandwich, blissfully ignorant of what was coming towards him. He noticed me and said, "Hey," to which I cleverly replied, "Happy good birthday!"

I'm not sure exactly what happened. My theory is evil gnomes. Somewhere between, "Have a good birthday" and "Happy birthday," my congratulations on having survived twenty-some years of life sounded like it was coming from the lips of someone who typically starts her morning off with an orange juice and battery acid cocktail.

He blinked a couple times. I prayed that he would think that his mind was just playing tricks on him, that I had just said something normal and not added or taken out necessary words for that sentence to make sense. This hope was shattered when Arielle burst into fits of laughter behind me.

I could see my conversation crashing and burning faster than an airplane made out of Twinkies and toothpicks and decided to bail. I quickly said, "Have day good!" made a full about-face and made a break for the exit.

I later found out that his nickname for me was "Yoda girl," just what I always wanted.

The morals of this story:

1. To guys: Girls get nervous too, and we will say dumb things, and we will feel like idiots for it.

2. When approaching someone you are attracted to, do not bring a friend. If it goes well, then you're fine. If it goes poorly that person will remind you of it until the day you die.

40. MUSIC MAN, HOW I LOATHE THEE

There are certain musicals that have crept into the collective hearts of the American populace, warming them from the inside like some fuzzy stuffed animal of Americana. *Cats, Cinderella, Fiddler on the Roof*, all pieces of American musical history and culture, and I detest them.

Don't get me wrong, I love musicals. I can watch *The Producers* or *Sweeney Todd* repeatedly (and have done so to the annoyance of many a roommate). But the classic, best loved, musicals of our culture mostly want to make me slam my head repeatedly in the lid of a grand piano.

Why this hatred for such beloved tales?

Believe me, if you ever worked as a lighting technician for any of them, you'd hate them as much as I do.

As a lighting technician, not only do you get to be there for the script read through, the endless rehearsals and every performance, but you often get to do so from the worst possible seat. If you're in the lighting booth, you can only see about 1/3 of the stage. If you're backstage you can only see or hear half the production. If you're in the spotlight bay, then you can see absolutely everything, but you can't hear worth a damn.

One day my boss came in more excited than a cat who has just discovered how to use a can opener. Bouncing up and down with, what I felt was sadistic, glee, he announced, "Gang, we're getting *The Music Man* account!"

Every last one of us replied with the same monotone, "yay."

As it turns out, there was a traveling off-Broadway production of the famous musical, and they had chosen our rather large stage to do their Northwest American premiere.

So, at the lovely hour of 4 am the next day, I found myself, with the rest of the stage crew, welcoming the actors, directors, musicians and harried looking road crew to our theater.

Unloading the set alone took 3 hours as the people who had originally packed everything into the back of the semi had apparently thought that at every stop in the road there would be a team of giants to help them unload. There was not a single box or set piece that weighed under 100 pounds, and so it fell mostly to me and about 3 other crew members, who weren't built like Olive from Popeye the Sailorman, to get things off the truck.

Let me tell you, you do not the know the true meaning of fear until someone yells, "It's loose! Get out of the way!" and you find yourself running for your life from a giant fountain on wheels.

Now, for this particular show we needed two spotlights. Sadly, one of our old faithful spotlights was on the fritz, and no amount of hitting it with a wrench was going to fix it this time. So in a mild panic, we had rented a spotlight for this show.

For those who think that if you've used one spotlight you've used them all, let me explain how wrong you are. Going from one followspot to another is often the difference between shooting a crossbow and a bazooka. This was the bazooka of spotlights. It weighed twice as much as the ones we used, the controls had obviously been designed by a NASA engineer and it stood on a stand, that at its lowest, put the spotlight about 5 inches above my head.

The other spotlight operator and I played rock, paper, scissors, and I lost. Stupid rock.

Now, because I was operating a new piece of equipment, I was supposed to have a little time to fiddle around with it to make sure that I understood the controls.

Then, disaster struck. The male lead in the performance got the stomach flu and so his understudy was needed to replace him. His understudy was 6 inches shorter. This meant that every costume had to be resized to fit him before the opening curtain at 6 pm. At this point it was 3 pm.

Now, aside from being a lighting technician, security and the occasional customer service person, I was also the resident seamstress. So when the lead seamstress for the production came out looking harried yelling, "Does anyone else in the damn building know how to sew!?" everyone took a giant step back and pointed at me. Lucky me.

A couple hours later we had gotten the sewing done, and I finally had my chance to try out the new lighting equipment. I donned my headset beside my fellow spotlight operator and over the headphones came the most disturbing voice I have ever heard.

The stage manager for the production sounded like the men from Monty Python whenever they cross dressed and pretended to be London housewives. High and screechy the man could have passed for the most annoying woman on the planet.

I later found out that my boss had actually said to him, "Wow, I hope you get over your cold soon."

And the man had replied, "This isn't a cold, this is my normal voice."

My fellow followspot operator in the booth, seeing my confused face, said, "Yeah, I'm with you, I've been listening to him for an hour and I want to jump out of this spotlight bay."

I was just getting some of the controls figured out when suddenly we had a call for stage and spotlights out, the audience was trickling in like very well dressed cattle.

The show began, though up in the spotlight bay we really couldn't tell. There were people running around on stage, and there was some dramatic pointing and we could faintly hear music, but for all we knew it was an interpretive dance of "Godzilla" set to elevator music.

"Ok, spotlight one, I'm going to need you to spotlight Susan in three, two, one!"

Have you ever had that dream where you showed up for a test and realized that you studied all the wrong chapters, or actually just have had that happen in real life? This was worse.

The stage manager apparently forgot that we had met the cast just today, and washed with stage lighting from on high, we were having problems discerning Susan from Greg the Forrest Troll.

I panicked, picked something that looked like a dress-clad figure and aimed that direction and flipped on the light. With the rest of the stage lights out I could now see that I had picked at least a lady and heard, "Good job spotlight one!"

I breathed a sigh of relief as my co-spotlight operator mumbled, "Lucky bastard."

I wasn't lucky for long, however. The stage manager kept yelling cryptic instructions over the headset, and anytime we asked for clarification shouted unhelpful things like, "Who is Gary, you ask!? Well, he's Gary!"

Despite this fact, my coworker and I managed to light the right people about 85 percent of the time. We finally approached intermission, and the leads got up on the stage to perform a very sonorous duet. Well, I suppose it was sonorous, up in the booth it sounded kind of like a sad Swedish Chef.

My headset crackled, "Followspot one, it is extremely important that at the end of this song you iris out completely and quickly."

For those who don't speak Spotlightese, there are multiple ways to take out the light from a spotlight on a stage, you can fade, you black out completely or you can iris, making the circle of light smaller and smaller until it vanishes completely. To do a quick iris out one must be able to both keep a 150 pound light steady, while twisting a nob the correct direction, while also not losing your composure and swearing loud enough for the audience below to hear.

It was at this moment that my 17 hours on the job brain realized something; I didn't actually know which direction of the nob would make the light smaller and which one would make the light bigger. I had had the light size setting pretty much the same the entire show, so I hadn't had to mess with it much. There was no way to test this without the audience wondering why the globe of light was suddenly changing size like some strange optical illusion.

Then it happened, the song came to an end and the stage manager called, "Lights out!"

I picked a direction and cranked. In the words of the ancient knight in *Indiana Jones and the Last Crusade*, "You have chosen poorly."

Suddenly a quarter of the stage was blown into relief by the power of a 1000-watt bulb at full capacity. Everyone on stage froze, the lead actress, the stagehands moving set pieces under cover of, what used to be, darkness, and the leading man who was tucking his shirt into his pants.

I scrambled and the light went out. However, the sudden motion unbalanced the followspot on its seesaw like stand and it came down and cracked me on the head.

I wasn't just seeing stars, I was seeing superstars; George Clooney and Cameron Diaz status stars. And in my ear was an accompanying soundtrack of high pitch angry screeching.

My coworker looked over at me on the floor and said, "Dude, he really does sound like a rabid, cross-dressing, chipmunk, doesn't he?

So what illuminating bits of knowledge can be learned from my brilliant failure?

1. Sometimes guessing is your only option, but if that fails, injure yourself to the point where no one will hold you responsible for your failure.

2. When giving directions, it is always important to remember that those who you are giving directions to don't actually live inside your head. You must be clear. No really, there are scientific studies to prove this.

3. If you are the head of a theater and wish to pick a musical that will make your stage crew hate you for eternity, just pick any one that says, "Dandy," "Gosh," or "Golly Gee" more than ten times in the script.

41. THE WEDDING OLYMPICS

I got my degree at a religiously founded, private university that was located exactly 45 minutes away from anywhere even slightly entertaining. The summation of these parts meant that in my college career I was subjected to more weddings than deep-fried Twinkies are sold at the Georgia State Fair.

Don't get me wrong, I believe that everyone has the inalienable right to find someone, date them for a month, then decide then and there they want to marry them (which happened more often than one would think at my college). I truly believe that marriage can be a wonderful thing; I just haven't felt extremely motivated to quasi-permanently attach myself to someone like a barnacle on the side of a ship quite yet.

However, because I wasn't as willing to dive into marriage like a blind swimmer who trusts that water has been added to the pool, I found myself on bridesmaid duty a ton.

Now, if you are a female and reading this, I understand that groaning noise, believe me we've all been there. If you're a guy reading this, or you happen to be near a female who is reading this, let me wipe that confused expression from your face and explain.

For men, being in a wedding means you take the groom to their bachelor's party then make sure at least one of you is sober enough the next morning to get everyone in suits and to the wedding.

However, if you are a bridesmaid, your responsibilities don't start the night before. Hell no! You will be involved with this wedding for months, maybe years, in advance.

You must attend the showers, get your dress fitted, spend copious amounts of time trying to find shoes that match the extremely odd bridesmaid dress color, only to discover that the lone shoes that match can only be ordered from a small village in Tibet, keep the bride calm, try to memorize half the guest list so you know who to run interference between... The list of the understood duties could go on for pages.

Every wedding is different too. If you're lucky, you will end up with a totally chill bride who just wants to have her wedding out on a lawn somewhere, wants all her bridesmaids to wear flip-flops and thinks the ceremony should take about fifteen minutes. This is the Holy Grail of weddings for a bridesmaid.

If you do not have the luck of a leprechaun, holding a rabbit's foot who has just found the end of a rainbow, then what you will get is what I will lovingly refer to as Belligerent Bliss.

These are the weddings in which the bride, the mother of the bride, an over possessive aunt or all of the above have decided that this wedding SHALL be the wedding of the century!

Yes, one must raise their arms into the Rocky Balboa stance while reading that last phrase out loud to get the full effect.

As was common in my college social circle, I soon found my presence not only being requested at the marriage of "such-and-such-a-person to such-and-such-a-person," but I was to be up front, holding a thorny bouquet wearing a dress that was the color of green, shiny swamp puke.

I am not a formal events type girl. I'm a, "has a one little black dress for all occasions type," so the prospect of throwing on yet another color that looked like a Crayola Crayon reject was a little less than thrilling. Add on the fact that the way this particular dress was stitched made my boobs look like I was trying to pull off Madonna's 80's cone look, and I can tell you right here and now I have never looked sexier.

By the way, for any males reading this, ugly bridesmaid dresses are intentional. This is because it is the bride's day, and no other girl will look prettier than her on her special day, damn it!

This particular wedding had four bridesmaids, two of whom were relatives of the bride, another random friend I had not met until the day of the wedding and my wise-ass self. The two relative bridesmaids were perfect angels of long-legged, blonde, dainty perfection. They walked on heels like they were floating through clouds of marshmallow fluff.

I am not that coordinated on heels, namely because I refuse to wear them unless bribed with beer, which, in reflection, may be the revolving door of failure. Let us also take into account that this dress was about 6 inches too long for my rather squat frame, and you have something less than graceful headed down the aisle.

However, my feminine failure was nothing compared to our fourth compadre. Standing at 5 feet flat, this pudding cup of drama let out her own insecurities by reminding everyone in the near vicinity that, while she was happy for the bride and groom, she was still single, and that just made weddings hard for her.

There are very few ways to put what I must say lightly, in fact saying that phrase is a rather bad pun in the situation. The Bitchy Bridesmaid was not small. Now, I am not necessarily small, myself. I am curvy and have spent years playing football, weight lifting and boxing, so please do not take my next comment as some kind of mean-spirited jab. This girl probably weighed 250 pounds plus and had about as much muscle as a baby field-mouse.

Ignoring the fact that she was cantaloupe-shaped, she had decided to opt for a style of bridesmaid dress that best compliments the type of girl who has never ever heard of sugar or carbohydrates, much less consumed any. The resulting look was a swamp-green shiny tube of toothpaste that a toddler had squeezed in the middle forcing the remaining goo to bunch at the top and bottom. Add a four-inch pair of heels she was definitely not used to walking in and you have the tottering Hummer wreck that was the Bitchy Bridesmaid.

The wedding was set up in a beautiful downtown location where one could tell, just by looking at the venue, that no one had ever crossed the building's threshold without a martini glass in hand or diamond cufflinks on their suit jacket.

To give you an idea of exactly how nice this place was, that during the chaos that later ensued, I asked one of the wait-staff for a beer and was promptly told, "We don't serve *that* beverage here. Would you like our *Somelongdrawnoutuppityname* wine, it tastes like some of the more… crude beers?"

I am not accustomed to high-class society. I am more of the does her hair and make-up in five minutes before dashing off to some event that she just remembered she promised to be at kind of girl. I once took manners lessons and nearly got myself removed from the course because I was challenging the other students to a duel with our knives.

Therefore, being plopped down in a super-fancy venue, like the one this wedding was being held at, for a day was a bit of a struggle, like trying to fit a rabid weasel in a matchbox, for me. I am proud to say, that until the actual wedding, I only said "shit-twinkle" once.

The wedding rehearsal went splendidly, the flower girl sprinkled flowers delicately while smiling and giggling down the aisle, I managed to both hold onto the groom's arm while not tripping over my heels or the dress down the aisle, the groom's vows were quoted better than Shakespearian quotation and the Bitchy Bridesmaid remained mostly silent and cheerful.

The wedding itself was a different matter altogether, much like the difference between a Disney Princess film and a movie about Hannibal Lector.

It all started with the flower girl, who, when faced with a crowd of adoring onlookers (mostly relatives), realized that show business wasn't all that it was cracked up to be and had a meltdown. Not only did she tear up and sob loud enough to shake a battleship apart, but the flower petals she was supposed to be sprinkling daintily found themselves being lobbed in all directions.

Eventually the child's father had to retrieve the girl, who at this point had pretty much gone into shock. Her sniffles could be heard like a bad omen for the rest of the ceremony as she was carried from the room, still frantically throwing flower petals.

I still managed to get down the aisle without face planting into carpet that probably cost more than any car I've ever owned. However, still a little off balance in the shoes I had bought not two days before the wedding, I wasn't prepared for the gust of wind that came through one of the charmingly open windows.

It wasn't a huge torrent of wind, it barely would have bothered a kitten. But these heels were far higher than I was used to wearing, and I was still trying to figure out how to hold my dress so that I didn't look like the green swamp cousin of Morticia Adams.

It's a good thing that golden decorative stand was there for me to steady myself on. It's a lesser good thing that the golden decorative stand had lit candles in it that were not firmly grounded.

I have no idea if anyone aside from me noticed that a candle thudded to the floor and rolled underneath my dress as I furiously, yet inconspicuously, stomped on the wick, but I do want to sincerely apologize to the staff of that venue if you were forever baffled by the random burn marks in your carpet.

The vows were said, but just like when you're forced to watch a documentary in school on grain production, time seemed to slow down. Both the bride and the groom, conscious of the fact that being nervous tends to speed one's speech up both were intentionally speaking more slowly. However, the more nervous they got, the slower they spoke and with more pauses were interjected.

By... the end... of the... ceremony... I... had... almost... planned... my... escape... to the... Island... of... Vigi.

Then, the ceremony was over, and the reception began. Sighing with relief that I had not ruined the bride's special day, as that would have resulted in being murdered with a cake server by her mother, I snuck off and put on some more comfortable shoes. It's not like anyone could see my feet now anyways.

When I came back I found the perkily perfect two bridesmaids looking at bridesmaid number four with an expression that would normally be reserved for, "Someone just broke into my car and left it full of religious pamphlets and a python, what do we do?"

I followed their confused gazes. First my eyes alighted on a wine glass, then another, and another, and by that point I was tired of moving slowly and snapped my attention directly to the now hiccupping and crying fourth member of our swamp-green brigade.

To say that she was drunk as a skunk in a funk would both be an understatement, and very hard to say seven times fast. In as little time as it takes to mix Jell-O powder with water, we were facing a very loud, very drunk person who had all the emotional coping abilities of a cracked out Scarlet from "Gone with the Wind."

The bride's mother, noticing the disturbance, mostly because you couldn't miss "the disturbance" if you were within a six-mile radius, made a beeline for us. She looked at the drunk one, then to the rest of us and in a whisper loud enough to be heard on the FBI wiretap two buildings over said, "Come on, help me get her to the car so we can get her back to my place. Quietly now!"

There was not a groomsman in sight. The other two bridesmaids together were about as big around as one of my biceps. We all three looked at each other for a second, but it was clear who was going to be making the magic happen here.

I got the inebriated chick's arm around my neck and we tottered towards the door that led to the parking lot, the mother of the bride following close behind. Both trying to keep myself from stepping on the super long dress and biffing it, and keeping the rather large person draped around me on her feet proved the be a task that I'm not entirely sure Hercules could have accomplished. Eventually I gave up all sense of decorum and stuck the skirt of the dress in my teeth.

After what felt like a hike across the Sahara Desert with a sack of iron potatoes on my back, we got the, still profusely sobbing, Bitchy Bridesmaid into the car.

No longer worried about having missed a day of weightlifting I climbed into the shotgun seat of the car as the mother of the bride took the wheel as we headed for their beautiful gigantic home.

The home we drove up to sat in the middle of a two-acre lot, with grass so green and lush it made you want to lie down in it immediately upon sight. Of course, that would probably make the landscapers a bit angry since they probably had to use rulers to cut the grass.

The interior of the house was white; white walls, white furniture, white carpet, even the light fixtures seemed to give off a cleaner, brighter form of luminescence. Hardwood floors paneled the hallways leading from laundry room, to the kitchen, to the living room, to the bathroom.

After a few more hefts I got the bridesmaid through the laundry room and kitchen, into the living room where I unceremoniously plopped her on the sofa. The mother of the bride surveyed the situation and oh so rightly surmised, "She should probably lie down, I'll go make sure the guest room is ready for her. Watch her, won't you?"

I nodded, tiredly as I plopped down on the sofa next to, but not too close to the girl who had had enough red wine to drown a fully-grown Saint Bernard. Suddenly, her head lolled towards me as she muttered those fateful words, "I think I'm gonna..."

I looked around in panic. We were in the center of a sea of white-carpet, with a long hardwood hallway leading to the nearest bathroom.

In a surge of strength that could only have been equated to someone telling the Incredible Hulk "Yo Mama" jokes, I grabbed her and propelled her over the white carpet, down the hall and to the bathroom. Carried by her momentum, we flew into the bathroom just as the Apocalypse struck.

Ok, Apocalypse could be an overstatement, but believe me, the result of the Bitchy Bridesmaid's boozy binge left the bathroom in a state that probably made whoever had to clean it up wish the world was ending.

I firmly believe there should be wedding Olympics. We could have events like the bouquet toss, angry relatives intervention and, of course, bridesmaid hefting (with light, middleweight and heavy classes of course). I would have won the gold medal.

In any case, I had an excellent excuse to get rid of that ugly-ass dress.

What bits of knowledge can we sift from our martini of experience?

1. Weddings are like a golf course designed by the Joker, there will be hidden hazards that may or may not include a live alligator and a time bomb.

2. When it comes to alcohol, know thy limits, unless you want an excellent excuse to not have to deal with the drunk people yourself, then have at it!

3. The possibilities of white carpet and Merlot can give a person Superwoman-like strength.

ABOUT THE AUTHOR

Allison Hawn was born in Idaho and has spent her life obtaining adventures. The daughter of a musician, she was brought up all over the United States with occasional dalliances into foreign lands. She holds a degree in psychology from Northwest Nazarene University in Nampa, Idaho, where she also had a weekly humor column with a small time newspaper *The Crusader*. *Life is a Circus Run by a Platypus* is her first creative published work. She currently resides in Spokane, Washington, where she works with homeless and at-risk youth, but calls a myriad of locations home.

Visit her blog at circusplatypus.blogspot.com

Made in the USA
San Bernardino, CA
07 September 2017